Health Psycl

Health and Nursing Studies for Diploma and Undergraduate Students

Health Psychology

Authors: Glenys Pashley and I C Henry

Health Ethics

Authors: I C Henry and Glenys Pashley

Health Care Research

Authors: I C Henry and Glenys Pashley

Health and Nursing Studies for
Diploma and Undergraduate Students

Health Psychology

by

Glenys Pashley and Christine Henry

Quay Publishing

Quay Publishing
11 Victoria Wharf
St George's Quay
Lancaster LA1 1GA

British Library Cataloguing in Publication Data
© Pashley, Glenys 1955-
Health psychology – (Health and nursing studies for diploma and undergraduate students)
1. Psychology
I. Title II. Henry, Christime 1946- III. Series
150

ISBN 1-85642-002-7

Printed in Great Britain by Lawrence Allen (Colour Printers) Limited, Weston-Super-Mare

Contents

Section 1

BACKGROUND AND INTRODUCTION

It is widely recognised today that health, social and paramedical students will become caring professionals by learning something of the way mind works, the course of personal development, change through the life cycle, social interaction in health and illness and an understanding of the psychological and social experiences of the person.

Psychology is often dealing with what appears to be commonsense. It is not so simple; judgements about mental or emotional impairment resulting from brain injury or disease and assessments of the psychological consequences of illness, surgery and treatment requires more than commonsense.

Psychology is controversial, different theorists arguing their own particular points of view; there are many different ways of interpreting and understanding human behaviour and experiences. It is not a question of certain theories being correct, but of using those theories that we feel are applicable and helpful in understanding the person and his/her experiences.

The patient is a person deserving respect. He/she is not simply a body nor a mere carrier of a condition or label, but an individual with a personality and forms of communication, thoughts, perceptions, feelings, needs, conflicts and expectations that have been nurtured throughout their experience to date. How the person views his/her illness will be influenced by these unique personhood features and it is up to the health professional to gain some understanding of these individual qualities, through applied psychological knowledge, in order to enhance individualised care for the person.

Health psychology is a relatively new area of psychology and is beginning to develop its own content, for example ideas about stress, pain, depression, anorexia nervosa, cancer, coronary heart disease, terminal illness and health behaviour. These experiences, unique to persons in a social context, whether in hospital or the community, can be more clearly understood through taking what is useful from the different approaches within psychology. It is argued that a sound and rigorous theoretical knowledge of psychological perspectives and concepts can enhance this understanding of a person's behaviour and experience of health and illness. **Cognitive** psychology can be useful for understanding how children, adolescents and adults perceive, thing and cope with their illness. **Social** psychology is functional for an understanding of attitudes towards health and illness, the development of interpersonal relationships and the skills of communication. **Educational** psychology can be useful in that a knowledge of learning theories are important for health educators and health professionals who may need to teach patients new skills.

Psychology has an historical development which has shaped its status and provided the variety of, sometimes contradictory, sometimes complementary, approaches within psychology. The focus of the first two chapters is to, briefly, introduce readers to the history of psychology and the different approaches. The remaining six chapters focus selectively on specific psychological concepts and how they might be useful to the health professional.

Chapter 1
Philosophical background and scientific status of psychology

Psychology is rooted within philosophy; hence it is important to have some understanding of the philosophical implications.

Philosophical psychology dates as far back as Aristotle and Plato who were concerned with such issues as the mind/body problem and consciousness. The **rationalists** maintained that persons could know things through reason and without experience, whilst the **empiricists** advocated that persons were a blank sheet of paper and could not acquire knowledge and concepts without experience. These two philosophical positions fit with particular approaches in psychology; the **cognitive** and the **behavioural** perspectives of the person, respectively. (More will be said about these links under Chapter 3 'Approaches in Psychology'.)

The notion of **dualism** implies that there is a distinction to be made between the mind and the body. The mind is held to be immaterial or non-physical and the body perceived as material or physical. One of the main problems evolving from this kind of distinction or separation of mind and body is, how do they or how can they interact when one is physical and the other is not? How can something influence nothing? If something like the mind is immaterial and therefore unobservable, does this imply non-existence? If the mind is material then where is it located? These are centuries-old philosophical questions which still relate to what is sometimes referred to in psychiatry, psychology and medicine/health as **psychosomatic disorders**, that is, physiological dysfunctions that result primarily from psychological processes. Perhaps the mind is really the same thing as the brain, although any meaningful answers to this dichotomy are more likely to be found in an examination of one's own values, beliefs and attitudes, and upon the conception of the person that one holds.

Different approaches to studying the person rest upon preconceived ideas of what the person is. Some psychological approaches prefer to understand a person's behaviour by utilising a scientific model, for example, the **positivistic** tradition in research employs scientific principles that treats persons as objects which can be observed, controlled, manipulated and measured. Wundt (1832–1920) founded the first psychological laboratory in Germany. The idea of a laboratory for studying behaviour fits with the general movement for the pursuit of science, but, if persons are more than simply passive objects, a scientific or positivistic form of inquiry does not fit.

Within psychology, positivism aims to be scientific in its research. Data is collected to test out hypotheses; the collection of that data involves observation and controlled experiments in order to be descriptive, objective and to make predictions and generalisations about a person's behaviour whilst he/she is separated from his/her usual surroundings. For positivists, it is important to discover cause-and-effect relationships. Within the health care field, this can generate some useful information, particularly in terms of physiological changes connected with illness or trials for drug treatment. However, conceiving the person in physiological terms only (medical model) reflects a reductionistic, materialistic and mechanistic view. Can we really treat persons as a combination of parts that can be isolated and fixed? What appears to be missing from the positivistic and scientific model of the person are unobservable phenomena which influence behaviour, for instance, motives, feelings, thoughts, intentions, decisions, personality and experience, that is, central personhood features.

Phenomenology is a philosophy and an approach to psychological research which attempts to take on board these features in relation to understanding persons. A phenomenological perspective emphasises the centrality of everyday life experience rather than studying the person in isolation and out of the social context. The whole person is seen to be important, not just the parts that need fixing. Phenomenology supports a humanistic viewpoint by looking at how the person perceives a situation; the intention is to understand rather than describe behaviour and experience. Persons are seen to be active in the sense that they influence their own environment as much as they are influenced by it (Henry, 1986), i.e. a person can influence their illness just as the illness can influence a person. In other words, credibility is given to the interactive relationship between physical, psychological, social and cultural aspects that comprise experience for the person. The meaning of that experience is unique, subjective and belongs to that person only. No attempt can be made to measure why Mrs Jones was in excruciating pain after her hysterectomy whilst Mrs Black was in substantially less pain. We can only try to understand why these two persons perceived and coped with their pain as they did. For example, Mrs Jones may have been experiencing more pain because she could no longer have children. Perhaps she felt that her womanhood had been taken from her or that she would be sexually unattractive. Possibly, these reasons would be added to the pain resulting from the surgery itself. The meaning that Mrs Jones attaches to her experience is what health professionals need to understand. As Carl Rogers (1972) implied, I am the expert of my 'self'.

Positivism treats everyone the same and assumes that what people are now, is what they always have been and always will be. Phenomenology recognises active individuality and, as Piaget (1896–1980) claimed, to understand a child and meet his/her needs, we must look at the world through his/her eyes. Therefore, to understand a patient's experience of illness and to develop individualised care, the health professional must perceive that experience through the eyes of the patient.

Discussion Points

1. What is your concept of the person?

2. Is the mind really the brain or is it something else?

3. How useful are positivism and phenomenology to the health professional?

4. What are the main methodological differences and problems for positivistic and phenomenological researchers? (See Polit and Hungler, 1987; Field and Morse, 1985.)

Useful Reading

Bunge, M. & Ardilo, R., (1987). *Philosophy of Psychology*, Springer Verlag

Field, P.A. & Morse, J.M., (1985). *Nursing Research: The Application of Qualitative Research*, Croom Helm

Gatchel, R.J. & Baum, A., (1983). *Health Psychology*, Random House

Medcof, J. & Roth, J., (1978). *Approaches to Psychology*, Open University Press

Polit, D.F., (1987). *Nursing Research: Principles and Methods*, Lippincott Co

Valentine, E.R., (1982). *Conceptual Issues in Psychology*, Allen & Unwin

Chapter 2
Approaches in psychology

There are several major approaches in psychology which make some attempt to explain a person's behaviour and experience. These different approaches tend to rest upon particular philosophical assumptions and beliefs which, in turn, account for the diverse range of possible explanations about behaviour and experience. A brief summary of some of the central perspectives follows. These are referred to throughout the text when dealing with specific psychological concepts.

(a) PSYCHOBIOLOGICAL PERSPECTIVE

The psychobiological perspective places emphasis upon explaining the psychology of the person in terms of their physiological structure and make-up. The main focus of this perspective is genetics, the brain and the central nervous system. Indeed, it is likely that the advocates of such an approach view the mind as being the same thing as the brain.

There is much research to support the links between physiology and psychology, for example, adrenalin increases when the person is excited, heart rate and blood pressure can increase if the person is stressed, and drugs can act as antidepressants. The cerebral cortex is the much-folded surface area of the brain. Persons are usually distinguished from other animals by the relatively vast cortical surface area of the brain which correlates with superior intelligence. However, the notion of intelligence is not easily defined and depends upon several other complex concepts for any level of understanding, for example, learning, memory, problem-solving, motivation, thought, language and experience in a social world. Certain areas of the cerebral cortex carry out specific functions. For example, the left hemisphere of the brain is more specialised for language and mathematical skills, whereas the right hemisphere is dominant for spatial and musical skills. However, there are large areas of the cortex where functions are less clear. The limbic system appears as a lining to the roof of the brain and surrounds the top of the brain stem. Broadly speaking, research has shown that the limbic system exercises some control over emotional and motivational behaviour. Damage to any part of this system appears to give rise to perceptual changes and disorders, such as an inability to distinguish visual cues, an impairment of recent memory and the disappearance of avoidance behaviour (for instance, when a person no longer appears to be afraid of painful stimuli). The question that needs to be asked is whether the changes in avoidance behaviour are necessarily the result of physiological changes or damage to the limbic system. It may be the case that the person has now come to terms with his/her illness or symptoms and feels that the time is right to consult the general practitioner or to disclose to others what he/she initially feared. In effect, the psychobiological perspective can be useful, in part, for enhancing our understanding of a person's behaviour. Physiological states are interactive with psychological states and do, indeed, relate to psychological concepts such as pain, stress and emotion. However, psychological concepts like these cannot be reduced to physical explanations alone. Further, there is the problem of whether physiological changes 'cause' psychological changes or whether psychological changes 'cause' physiological changes. For example, the effects of placebos on perceived symptoms: a person can take a tablet believing that it will relieve pain; the belief rather than the contents of the tablet may be effective.

Discussion Points

1. How far has your own experience of illness influenced your behaviour, personality or mood?

2. When you feel anxious, what physiological changes accompany this anxiety?

3. What does the psychobiological perspective tend to ignore in its attempt to explain a person's behaviour?

Useful Reading

Bakal, D.A., (1979). *Psychology and Medicine*, Tavistock

Blundell, J., (1975). *Physiological Psychology*, Methuen

Medcof, J. & Roth, J., (1979). *Approaches to Psychology*, Open University Press

Niven, N., (1989). *Health Psychology*, Churchill Livingstone

(b) BEHAVIOURISM TO NEOBEHAVIOURISM

Behaviourism is rooted within seventeenth century British empiricism in the sense that all ideas and knowledge are acquired empirically through the senses. In other words, all that we know is a result of what we have learned; we are not born with any knowledge.

Behaviourism concentrates on the external and observable rather than the internal and unobservable features of the person; hence terms like mind, consciousness and the subjective self are inappropriate and non-functional. Behaviour is seen to be the result of an individual learning to **respond** appropriately to **stimuli** presented in the environment, and that appropriate responses are **conditioned** and **reinforced**.

Behaviourism is concerned with the role of the external environment in shaping and governing our actions; factors controlling human behaviour reside within the environment rather than within the individual. In effect, persons are seen to be environmentally determined, thus leaving no room for people to choose freely how to respond.

The early behaviourists like Pavlov (1849 – 1936), Thorndyke (1874 – 1949), Watson (1878 – 1958) and Skinner (1904 – 1989) grounded their theory in the principles of learning and argued that the proper subject matter of psychology was observable overt behaviour. In a sense, these early behaviourists put a lid on the box of internal processes and declared, for so-called scientific purposes, that it was empty. For this reason, behaviourism is otherwise referred to as stimulus – response (S – R) psychology and is often criticised for missing the 'O', that is, concern for the **organism** or person. If we learn everything simply through responding to stimuli presented to us in the environment, how are creative thoughts explained? Can we ignore the influence of thoughts, intentions, motives, purposeful behaviour simply because they are unobservable? Pain is not an observable phenomenon; it is something that is subjectively experienced and which influences our behaviour but we certainly would not deny it.

The neo-behaviourists like Hull (1884–1952) and Tolman (1886–1959) recognised the need to take into account the **organism** and its internal states, such as drives, needs, goals and purposes which underlie behaviour. In effect, the principles of learning were combined with internal features of the person and S–R psychology became S–O–R psychology. The introduction of the 'O' or organism as a concern for psychologists links to the **cognitive** approach which essentially focusesd upon the internal processes or features of the person, for example, thoughts, intentions, motives, memory, language development and problem-solving strategies. However, before giving an overview of the cognitive approach to psychology, it is useful to provide some information on **behavioural therapy**, a method or 'treatment' based on the theoretical assumptions of behaviourism and which makes some attempt to help people **learn** to **change** their behaviour.

(c) BEHAVIOURAL THERAPY

By definition, behavioural therapy is treatment for observable behaviour. It is a systematic way of changing the environment and people in order to provide new learning experiences. The two types of learning techniques that are used in behaviour therapy are **classical** and **operant**. An alternative word for learning is **conditioning;** hence these learning techniques are often referred to as classical and operant conditioning.

Behaviour therapy has been used to help patients/clients/individuals with a wide range of problems, symptoms and odd responses. Such problematic responses tend to be due either to an excess or a deficit in response. Excess problems include behavioural responses that already exist and which the individual displays but, somehow, they prevent that individual from being entirely independent, for example, frequent screaming, compulsive and repetitive movements or speech. Deficit problems would be behaviours that an individual had not learned to do, but, if they had, then they would function more independently, for example, lack of language and communication skills, inability to go outside the house.

'Behaviour' is what people **do**. It includes what we can see or **observe** another person doing, for example, opening a door or sitting in a corner. The important point is that we only call something 'behaviour' when we can **observe it**. So day-dreaming or thinking are **not** behaviours. These things could only be guessed at on the basis of behaviour alone. Such a guess would be a **subjective** definition of behaviour. 'Subjective' means that we, the observers, are **interpreting** what someone is feeling or thinking on the basis of what we can see. In contrast, an **objective** behavioural definition does not need guesswork. So all observers can **agree** on what behaviour took place. This agreement allows us to **accurately record** behaviour. In making an 'interpretation' we are being **subjective**. We have gone beyond what we can **observe**. It is only when we describe behaviour in **objective** terms that we can all **agree** on what has taken place. If we tried to record things like 'confidence', 'hostility' or 'hallucinating' we would no doubt get a lot of disagreement between observers. This is because they are **subjective** definitions. If instead we define these behaviours **objectively** we would probably improve agreement.

Another feature of behaviour is that it is something we do **in the environment**. We behave, or emit responses in order to **act on** the things or people around us. Such behaviour is called 'operant'. 'Behaviour' then is a way of acting on the **environment**. That is to say, we 'operate' on the environment by emitting **responses**. **Reflexes**, that is responses that are **elicited by** the environment, are different. They occur when something **happens to** a person. That person does not have control over the reflex. With operant behaviour, the individual is in control, attempting to influence the environment. When a behaviour, or response, is **elicited** we mean that the environment **operates** on them. They are passive and simply react.

Classical conditioning is a process of learning whereby new or conditioned stimuli can be associated with old stimuli. For this to occur, the new stimuli must occur immediately before the old; the response then follows. In this way, events or cues are paired together or associated and, in turn, the new cues can elicit old responses. The central aspects of classical conditioning are a reflex, a neutral stimulus and timing. A reflex is a stimulus **and** a response. The response is elicited by the stimulus. A neutral stimulus is any cue that does not elicit the response **before** conditioning. A few seconds gap between the old stimulus and the neutral or new stimulus can prevent learning, so the neutral stimulus must occur immediately before the old one. The association between old and new stimuli is weak if time is allowed to pass.

It was a Russian psychologist, Pavlov (1849 – 1936), who demonstrated how learning by classical conditioning took place. The central point is that things occurring almost simultaneously are associated with each other and trigger the old or established response. The old stimulus he referred to as **unconditioned**, the new or associated stimulus he called **conditioned**. The importance of Pavlov's work lies in his claim that the old stimulus or unconditioned stimulus can be used to create a new or conditioned stimulus which can have the effect of controlling recurring problems.

In contrast to classical conditioning, which is to do with learning new **cues** for old responses, operant conditioning concerns how people acquire **new** behaviours. It was Skinner (1904 – 1989), an American psychologist, who developed and outlined the principles of operant learning. Behaviour is seen to be controlled by its **consequences**. There are four distinct kinds of consequence: **reward, punishment, time-out** and **escape.** Reward, otherwise referred to as **reinforcement**, and suggesting that behavioural responses are strengthened, is the consequence most often used in behavioural therapy. Rewards might include edible items, such as sweets, manipulable objects, like games and toys, social comment, like praise, or conditioned items, such as money and tokens.

There are a number of important points with regard to rewarding behavioural responses:

1. The strongest reward ought to be used
2. This should be given immediately following the sought-after response.
3. Initially, a reward should be given each time the response is made.
4. A combination of rewards should be given at the same time, for instance, whilst praising a patient money or sweets or cigarettes can be given
5. Rewards should be consistent, that is, the consequences for a sought-after response should be repeated.

Reward and escape serve to strengthen a response (escape might involve removing an unpleasant stimulus), whilst time-out and punishment weaken a response (time-out might involve removing a pleasant stimulus and punishment involves giving an unpleasant stimulus, for example, electric shock treatment).

It is essential that these four kinds of consequences are defined and assessed on the basis of their effects, because what may be an unpleasant stimulus for one individual may be a pleasant stimulus for another individual.

The are four ways of helping an individual to respond: shaping, prompting, modelling and fading.

SHAPING is a way of gradually helping the individual to make the correct or appropriate response and means giving rewards only when each attempt at the response is better than the previous one.

PROMPTING is a more direct way of helping an individual to respond through physical, verbal or gestural actions on the part of the therapist, for example, physically holding the person and guiding their movements, verbally telling the individual to do something or indicating through action what needs to be done.

MODELLING is a precise demonstration by the therapist so that the individual can **imitate** the action

FADING implies a phasing out of promptful help and rewards, in other words, aids to responding are gradually removed. For example, the frequency of rewards can be lessened by rewarding every other response rather than each and every response.

There is much literature on behaviourism and behavioural therapy. The above account serves only to introduce readers to the central terms underpinning the theory and its application. Several studies can be cited which use some form of behaviour modification or therapy in order to demonstrate its acclaimed success. Engel (1972) has reported that a group of people with high blood pressure were trained to lower this physiological response through **biofeedback**. Biofeedback is the general name given to training techniques that enable some physiological responses, like heart rate and blood pressure, to come under voluntary control. It rests upon the principles of operant conditioning but is particularly concerned with the conditioning of responses controlled by the autonomic nervous system. The patient watches a visual display of his/her blood pressure and is requested to increase or decrease the 'score'. The visual information is also transformed into an auditory signal which lets the patient know further of any increase or decrease (a form of reinforcement). The patient eventually uses the sound to monitor his/her performance. He/she can also be asked to imagine calm and drowsy situations which can have the effect of lowering blood pressure.

Wolpe (1958) reports on the use of **systematic desensitisation** to alleviate fear responses. A patient is first requested to list the contexts in which he/she experiences fear. These contexts are then rank ordered by the patient from the least to the most feared. He/she is trained to relax or relaxation is induced through drugs and when this is achieved the stimulus at the bottom of the hierarchy is presented to him/her either in reality or through imagination. When the patient is able to cope with this stimulus without any fear or anxiety the next one in the sequence is presented. Eventually the patient is able to tolerate what was the most feared object or situation.

Modelling is a similar technique to systematic desensitisation. In this case, the patient observes a model behaving in a non-anxious manner in the same fear-provoking situation that presents the patient with uncontrollable anxiety. This observation serves to lower the patient's fear and anxiety and allows the patient to imitate the model's coping behaviour. This procedure is based on the experimental findings of Bandura (1965) and has been effective in reducing hospital admission stress in children who have been shown a film of a cheerful child entering hospital, having an operation and returning home.

There are, however, a number of concerns regarding the assumptions, premises and ethical implications of behaviourism and behavioural therapy. These ought to be borne in mind and discussed thoroughly.

1. It is an approach which treats people objectively or as being machine-like.

2. The role of the environment is seen to determine or control behaviour and, in this sense, there is no room for a person acting on the basis of free-will.

3. An attempt is made to change behaviour. Value judgements are implicit, for example, who decides what behaviour needs changing; where, how and when should this change occur?

Useful Reading

Coleman, J.C., (1977). *Introductory Psychology: A Textbook for Health Students*, Routledge & Kegan Paul
Dobson, C.B. & Hardy, M. et al., (1988). *Understanding Psychology*, Weidenfeld & Nicholson
Fairburn, S. & Fairburn, G., (1987). *Psychology, Ethics and Change*, Routledge & Kegen Paul
Gross, R., (1989). Psychology: *The Science of Mind and Behaviour*, Hodder & Stoughton
Medcof, J. & Roth, J., (1978). *Approaches to Psychology*, Open University Press
Valentine, E.R., (1982). *Conceptual Issues in Psychology*, Allen & Unwin

(d) COGNITIVE PERSPECTIVE

The cognitive perspective within psychology is essentially concerned with the internal processes of the person, for example, thoughts, intentions, memory, attention, problem-solving and perception. In other words, it is those aspects of the person that can only be inferred rather than directly observed. Research on cognitive psychology may focus on how individuals utilise different thinking strategies for problem-solving, how well different individuals store and recall information from memory and how perception of illness can influence coping strategies.

A cognitive perspective to understanding the person is primarily concerned with cognitions rather than affective or behavioural factors. However, it is important to be aware that there is an interrelationship between these cognitive, affective and behavioural factors. For example, a person can think and believe that he/she is ill, subsequently feel depressed and begin to socially withdraw from other people. Conversely, old age and infirmity could prevent the person from socialising with others; this might lead to feelings of loneliness, isolation and sadness and, in turn, to a low self-concept.

Discussion Points

1. What signs and symptoms do you attend to and which do you ignore?

2. How well do you remember previous experiences of illness – is the memory of your illness more or less vivid than the actual experience of it?

3. What is the relationship between thought and emotion – are thoughts rational and logical and emotions irrational and illogical?

Useful Reading

Bornstein, M.H. & Lamb, M.E., (1988). *Perceptual, Cognitive and Linguistic Development*, LEA Publishers

Butterworth, G. & Light, P., (1982). *Social Cognition*, Harvester Press

Gatchel, R.J., Baum, A. & Krantz, D., (1989). *An Introduction to Health Psychology*, Newbery Record Awards

(e) PSYCHOANALYTICAL PERSPECTIVE

The psychoanalytical approach to psychology derives from the work of Freud (1870–1937). The Freudian model has also been referred to as **psychodynamic**, essentially because it views a person as an energy system: a set of psychological forces that drive people to behave in certain ways. These forces are biologically based instinctual drives and the central ones of any significance to Freud were sexual, aggressive, life and death instincts.

Freud placed great emphasis upon the conflict between the desire to express these instincts and society's conventions and restrictions. Conflicts arise because these instincts are inhibited by social factors and, because they are inhibited, are repressed in the unconscious mind. As far as Freud was concerned, the key to human behaviour lies in the unconscious mind and the past experiences of the person. He proposed that the structure of the mind comprised three parts, the **id**, the **ego** and the **superego**. The id wants what it wants and it wants it now, the ego is aware of reality and so acts as some kind of arbitrator by controlling the id's desires to fit into that reality and the superego endorses the ego's recommendations by reminding the id that moral and social values ought to prevent us from behaving in particular ways. Freud claimed the first five years of development in childhood were crucial; particular stages of development are passed through which very much influence what we are in later life.

Much more detail about Freudian theory will be given in the chapter focusing on personality. For present purposes it is important to note that there is some similarity with the views of the behaviourists in the sense that both reflect an element of determinism. Internal determinism is reflected in Freudian theory through the emphasis and dependency upon biological instincts, whilst behaviourism purports external determinism, that is, behaviour is conditioned by environmental factors. There are also fundamental differences between Freudian and behaviouristic theory in that the behaviourists are only concerned with what is observable, measurable and concrete, whereas Freudian theory is shot through with abstract terms and the notion of a mind, rather than a brain, which is unobservable, unlocatable and inaccessible to direct experiences.

Discussion Points

1. Can you identify any instinctual drives that influence your behaviour?

2. Are there things that you would like to do but can't because it is not socially acceptable or because you know it is wrong – have you repressed these feelings?

3. Can you recall any childhood experiences that have influenced what you are now, for example, have childhood experiences of illness affected your perception of illness, how you react and cope with illness or had any bearing upon your role as a health professional?

Useful Reading

Fairburn, S. & Fairburn, G., (1987). *Psychology, Ethics and Change*, Routledge & Kegan Paul

Hayes, N. & Orrell, S., (1987). *Psychology: An Introduction*, Longman

Medcof, J. & Roth, J., (1978). *Approaches to Psychology*, Open University Press

Valentine, E.R., (1982). *Conceptual Issues in Psychology*, Allen & Unwin

(f) HUMANISTIC PERSPECTIVE

The humanistic viewpoint has moved away from the notion that persons are just observable behaviour, or simply biological parts, or driven by the instincts of sex and aggression. For psychologists such as Abraham Maslow (1908–1970) and Carl Rogers (1902), persons are seen to have positive motives that are good and the natural tendency for the person is towards full development, **self-actualisation** as Maslow puts it. The term 'good' refers to an evaluative and ethical judgement about human nature rather than being a purely descriptive term, very much like Tolman's notion of purposive behaviour. It evokes questions such as, 'What do we mean by good?' and, 'What reasons do we have for judging something as good?' Value is placed upon a side of human nature in that persons are active and have positive motives to achieve. This indicates notions of intentionality and self-awareness.

Maslow assumed human nature to be essentially good, creative and capable of healthy growth. He concentrates on healthy rather than disordered personality. According to Maslow, human needs can be represented through an hierarchical pattern or scheme. As each level is satisfied, the next level predominates until the highest level of self-actualisation is attained. There is a requirement for a **self-concept**. This refers to the concept of a person as more than the sum of parts, aspects of self-reflection and self-knowledge being important. The self-concept becomes a central feature of the unity of the concept of the person and recognition of the person as an internal active agent.

At the lowest level, basic physiological needs, such as food and warmth, require satisfaction in order for the individual to survive. Following this basic level is a concern for safety which involves needs for security and protection. When the safety level is gratified, there emerges a level of belonging and love, for such needs as group identification and acceptance, along with desires for affectionate relationships. If satisfaction is reached, there follows a level of esteem involving needs for adequacy, competence, mastery, freedom and independence, with social desires for status and prestige. Finally, an individual reaches the level of self-actualisation which equates to the full development of the person.

Rogers pioneered client-centred psychotherapy and his humanistic approach is built around only a few basic concepts. Rogers outlines several important features of the person and suggests that in-built into human nature is a basic set of values which have moral implications and refers to this as an **organismic valuing process.** Rogers talks of a need for positive regard implying that persons find it necessary to gain the respect of others and this leans towards social needs emphasising interaction as a feature of the person. A person has a **phenomenal field** which is viewed as his/her own unique perception of the world and the **self-concept** is important; part of a person's phenomenal field is a perception of an ideal self. Rogers points out that for psychological health, the real world, the self and the ideal self must be compatible. Sometimes a person's view of reality does not correspond to the actual reality. If some incompatibility occurs, then the person will experience what he termed incongruence. Rogers conceives of the total personality, i.e. the whole person, as comprising the self 'structure' and experience. If the self structure includes experience then the person can be assumed to be congruent. If, on the other hand, the self structure excludes experience, then incongruence results in psychological ill health. The importance of the organismic process is emphasised and Rogers, in a similar way to Maslow, calls this the actualising tendency because it allows growth, curiosity and fuels both drives and motives.

The humanistic psychologists claim that both behaviourism and Freudian theory are dehumanising and mechanistic. The person cannot be reduced to being biologically or environmentally determined, rather the person should be viewed as a whole and, therefore, biological, social, cognitive and emotional influences should be taken into account when attempting to understand a person's behaviour and experience. For the humanists, the acknowledgement of a conscious mind hints at a less organic and determined view of the person. The self-concept is construed as a key feature of the person and indicates self-reflection and direct subjective knowledge of oneself. Human nature is held to be good, positive and to reflect free-will and there is a phenomenological aspect in that an individual's experience is seen to be central.

Discussion Points

1. What would represent self-actualisation for you personally?

2. What is the concept that you have of yourself?

3. When you are ill, what do you feel are your most important needs?

Useful Reading

Heaton, J.M., (1979). Theories in psychotherapy. In *Philosophical Problems in Psychology*, ed. N. Bolton, Methuen & Co.

Medcof, J. & Roth, J., (1978). *Approaches to Psychology*, The Open University Press

Valentine, E.R., (1982). *Conceptual Issues in Psychology*, Allen & Unwin

These first three chapters have attempted to give some foundation to the status of psychology and an overview of the central principles underpinning the different approaches within psychology.

From a health professional's point of view no rigid adherence to any one theory will adequately explain a patient's behaviour and experiences whilst he/she is ill. It is likely that any knowledge from a combination of approaches can facilitate an understanding of a patient's reactions and individual ways of coping. In this sense, a phenomenological perspective is useful to the health professional. It stresses that the health professional takes what is useful from all of the available knowledge and considers the person in his/her surroundings, taking into account past experiences and the inner self. Health professionals ought to regard their patients as being active and interactive with the social world, and that individualised care entails understanding each person and how they view the world and their experience within that world through their eyes.

The following chapters focus on selective concepts within psychology and show how different approaches attempt to define, explain and understand these concepts. For example, the behaviourists would advocate that thought is really language, the cognitive psychologists would view language and thought as quite distinct, and humanistic or phenomenological psychologists would claim that language and thought are best understood in terms of the meaning that an individual attaches to particular words or thoughts.

Section 2

DEVELOPMENT

Developmental psychology is concerned with examining the physical, social, emotional, moral and cognitive development of the child, through lifespan, to old age. Development is also very much dependent upon the complex interplay between genetic and environmental factors that influence person. Although it is difficult to assess just how much influence each factor has on development, a central concern is to map out some of the changes that do occur in individual development. The following three chapters are specifically concerned with the young child in terms of his/her cognitive development, acquisition of language and thought, the effects of deprivation and the influence of illness on a child's experience and subsequent development.

Chapter 3
Early experience and later psychological developments

What is meant by development? Developmental psychologists usually associate development with the age-related changes that occur in behaviour, and offer different explanations for the processes underlying such changes. Some of the central issues of concern for developmental psychologists focus upon questions such as:

- Are there clearly distinguishable stages or critical periods of human development?
- What characteristics and capabilities does the child have at birth and how do these influence later development?
- Is development in adulthood different from development in childhood?
- Are different aspects of development interrelated, for example, what is the relationship between social, emotional, moral, cognitive and behavioural development?
- How influential is heredity and the environment in development? This is the nature/nurture debate.

CAUSES AND CONDITIONS OF DEVELOPMENT: THE INTERACTION OF NATURE AND NURTURE

What governs the course and rate of the sorts of physical development? To answer this, one must return to the origin of the human individual as a single living cell resulting from fertilisation. The fertilised ovum will proceed to divide and multiply itself over and over again, with sets of cells acquiring specialised characteristics and functions. The whole process is guided by a blueprint contained in the nucleus of each cell and replicated as new cells are generated through the division process known as mitosis. This plan or blueprint, the genotype, is conveyed by twenty-three pairs of chromosomes in the cell nucleus. Each chromosome contains many genes which carry the information that will affect development of particular characteristics in the organism being formed. This genetic material consists of strings of complex molecules (DNA). As a result of meiosis, half the chromosomes in the fertilised ovum originally came from the gametes of each parent. The number of possible combinations in this random process are infinitely large, and biologists say that this is one of the main evolutionary advantages of sexual reproduction. The main point emphasised is that the mechanisms of heredity produce both continuity and change, similarity and differences between parents and offspring.

Like an engineering blueprint, the genotype has been applied to something and the continuing dynamic existence of living systems requires input and exchange of energy and nutriment from the surrounding environment. It is obvious that such inputs might influence the course of the organism's development. Physical development is essentially due to interaction of heredity (nature) and environment (nurture): the two may be distinguished conceptually but cannot be separated in reality. The phenotype (what we actually see) is the result of the conjoint action of the genotype and environmental influences. The psychologist, Donald Hebb, puts this well by likening the development to the concept of 'area': any area is two dimensional and cannot be reduced to one; any rectangular area is seen as a multiplicative function of length and breadth.

Sometimes, it has been stated that the genetic blueprint sets the upper limits to development, so that, if one genotype specifies the height of six feet under the optimum conditions of nutrition etc., no amount of extra food or vitamins would get one taller than six feet. There are two important points to be made here. First, we cannot examine the genotypes or genetic potential. Until we can actually examine the genotypes independently of the phenotypes they govern, then such statements about limits tell us nothing. We don't know what an individual's genotype is, whatever the phenotype presented by his/her parents. Secondly, environmental influences may also limit development, for instance, chronic malnutrition can stunt growth permanently.

Instead of being tempted to simplify the causes of development into a one-dimensional view, favouring either heredity or environment alone, we should be more interested in discovering the particular interactions that govern specific aspects of development and in relating them to the range of alternative influences we may have at our disposal. Such interactions can vary from relatively straightforward to extremely subtle, and, within them, the weight of heredity as opposed to environmental or potential intervention may vary considerably. It should be admitted that calling the genotype the blueprint tends to make things seem static; it is true that some genetic control acts very constantly through life (skin growth), but the plan is carried by every cell and may cause particular developments only at given points in the developmental sequence. Puberty is clearly an example of such age-linked genetic expression. Closely related to this notion of critical periods is imprinting. Some ethologists (e.g. Lorenz, 1952) have discovered a similar imprinting in animals, whereby a certain response, often involving attachment, will be applied to objects encountered at a particular time. For example, geese will show sexual behaviour towards the first thing they encounter during a short period, starting a few hours after they are born. There is considerable controversy over the existence of true imprinting in humans, but often-quoted types of critical periods include toilet training and learning to walk. It has been shown that training is useless until the nerve paths have matured, at around two years for bladder control and just under one for walking.

It also needs to be pointed out that the term 'environment' is rather an unfortunate term, in that it may suggest a passive organism undergoing influence from without. While the influences that affect development from the moment of conception onwards may well be called environment, much will depend on how the organism actively responds to particular conditions (using what it has gained from the totality of such previous interactions).

We are now in a position to put forward a more specific definition of some important, but often loosely-used, terminology in this area. Maturation should be used to refer to physical and psychological events and changes that depend mainly on genetic programming. Growth corresponds to this aspect, indicating the unfolding of structures specified by the genotype. Thus, puberty is obviously a clear example of a maturational event. Development refers more broadly to change that tends to happen with increasing age, where one is not sure to what extent or how directly such changes depend upon maturation. For instance, the development of large muscles clearly requires certain levels of exercise as an experiential factor interacting with heredity. The maturational and developmental distinction can be particularly relevant to cognitive development, where intellectual development can be influenced by experience. Developmental psychologists study all the psychological processes to see how they develop and change throughout life. Not only do they study the unfolding of perceptual and intellectual processes in infancy, but also in childhood, adolescence and through to old age. The point is that physical maturation and decline affect behaviour and, therefore, some knowledge of physical development is vital.

Early experience and later psychological developments

Development in the early part of life is very rapid. There is more obvious change in a relatively short period of time than there is later on; therefore, a year's experience in early childhood seems to count for more than a year's experience later on.

Early research into the deprivation experiences of children indicated a lasting and damaging effect upon their development. Much of the work in this area has been stimulated by Bowlby's claim (1951) that the young child should experience a warm, intimate and continuous relationship with his/her mother or permanent mother substitute if his/her mental health and subsequent development was not to be endangered. Failure to form an emotional bond before the age of two and a half would permanently impair the ability to make social/emotional relationships in later life and, in extreme cases, could lead to the syndrome known as 'affectionless psychopathy'. Bowlby saw a child's attachment to its mother as stemming from a survival instinct and that if bonding did not occur because of maternal deprivation, then irreversible social and intellectual damage would occur. Bowlby concluded from his studies; "There is a very strong case indeed, for believing that prolonged separation of a child from his/her mother (or mother substitute) during the first five years of life stands foremost among the causes of delinquent character development."

One problem with this study is that it is retrospective and looks only at a selected sample who have presented problems; many children who have experienced temporary separations show no lasting effects. Secondly, Bowlby had not looked closely at **why** the children had been separated. This is crucial as it is likely that, in many cases, separation was brought about by a bad family situation, which itself would be damaging. Rutter (1971) has since shown that delinquency is related to discord and distortion of relationships in the family rather than separation as such (and Bowlby has recognised this in later writings). Thirdly, there was no long-term follow-up which would be necessary to substantiate any claim that effects are permanent. Antisocial behaviour often ceases when former delinquents marry and have 'something to lose'.

Goldfarb (1943) carried out a retrospective study comparing a group of children who had been fostered soon after birth with a group who had not been fostered until they were three (the first three years were spent in an institution). Goldfarb looked at their development at age 10–14 (there were fifteen children in each group) and found the late-fostered group to have lower attainment in IQ, speech, and social and emotional development (e.g. they found it more difficult to make relationships). He tried to match the ability with the circumstances of the natural mothers and also the foster homes, and concluded that the differences in development must be attributed to the early 'maternal deprivation' of the late-fostered group. As with the Bowlby study, a major criticism is that we do not know **why** one group was deprived in this way; why were some children not fostered immediately? Could there have been problems in the family histories or with the children themselves which affected the decision not to foster until later? A problem with retrospective studies is that the relevant information may have been forgotten or distorted with time.

Spitz (1945) compared four groups of babies: two groups of babies in families; one group being cared for by their own mothers in prison; and one group of 'foundlings' in a very poor institution. All groups made good progress except the institutionalised babies who showed a steady decline over the first year of life. The babies were cared for by grossly overworked nurses (one nurse to 8–12 babies) and normally had adult attention only for feeding and changing (when possible 'propped' bottles were used for feeding so that contact was minimal). There was little stimulation in the form of toys or even things to look at (cots had covered sides). Twenty-one of the children were followed up when they were aged 2–4; at this time, only five could walk unassisted, only nine could eat alone with a spoon, and only one could dress herself. Spitz was aware of the fact that all forms of stimulation were lacking but regarded maternal deprivation as the key factor.

Researchers nowadays would be much more likely to give due weight to perceptual and language deprivation as well as social and emotional deprivation.

Bowlby's work on maternal deprivation had an immediate impact on educationists and policy makers and was widely quoted and misquoted. Among the benefits were a trend towards greater sensitivity to the needs of young children, improvements in institutional care and the introduction of unrestricted hospital visiting. On the other hand, Bowlby's work was used to reinforce the idea that the mother's place is always in the home. Separation from the family was regarded as damaging and some authorities felt that bad homes were preferable to good institutions. This produced a situation where children's officers were reluctant to remove children, even from very bad homes. It was considered that late adoptions (after the age of three) were unlikely to be successful and many children who might have been placed were not even put forward for adoption. Day nurseries and nursery schools also came in for attack. A World Health Organisation Expert Committee (to which Bowlby had reported in 1951) concluded that the use of day nurseries inevitably caused "permanent damage to the emotional health of a future generation". Baers (1954) claimed that the normal growth of children is dependent on the mother's full-time occupation in the role of child-rearer and that "anything that hinders women in the fulfilment of this mission must be regarded as contrary to human progress". Margaret Mead, writing in the same year, noted that these statements were made by men and dismissed them as just another attempt by men to shackle women to the home. People like Baers had ignored the fact that Bowlby's arguments were derived almost entirely from studies of children who were completely separated from their families, often in institutions, and that the reason for their separation was, in many cases, a bad family situation. Bowlby himself had made a distinction between the circumstances of these children and the children of working mothers and had concluded, in at least one article, that partial daily separation is relatively harmless, given the existence of a close emotional bond. Other better designed and/or more carefully interpreted research has given a much modified picture of the effects of early deprivation.

In the 1930s (USA), Skeels was asked to remove two poorly functioning babies, aged 13 and 16 months, from an orphanage. He placed them in an institution for the mentally retarded where they became the objects of attention and stimulation by retarded women with mental ages of about nine. Their development was greatly accelerated and, at the age of three and a half, they were placed in adoptive homes. Skeels and Dye (1939) then did the same thing with thirteen other retarded orphanage children and selected a contrast group with initially higher ability who remained in orphanages. The same thing happened as before – the experimental group improved rapidly and were placed for adoption. Long-term follow-up showed that members of the experimental group generally did rather well in terms of jobs and personal relationships. Between them they had twenty-eight children with a normal range of IQs (86 – 125) and school progress. With one exception, outcome for members of the contrast group was uniformly poor: they either remained institutionalised or achieved only low-grade jobs; only two married and only one had children. The exception, who did as well in adulthood as those in the experimental group, was a child who, because of a sensory defect, had been removed from the orphanage to a much more stimulating residential special school. This study is often misleadingly quoted to emphasise the importance of **early** experience – it is important to remember that these groups had different experiences **throughout their childhood and adolescence** – the experimental group had early extensive stimulation by the retarded but attentive women and then further continuing stimulation in their adoptive homes, whereas the contrast group spent the whole period in the unstimulating environment of the orphanage.

The case of 'Isabelle' was reported independently by Mason (1942) and Davis (1940, 1947), 'Anna's' case was reported only by Davis. Both children were discovered in the 1930s in the USA, having been isolated until the age of six. Isabelle was illegitimate and had been locked in an attic with her deaf-mute mother by the mother's father. When they eventually escaped Isabelle was found to be very retarded – she was also in poor physical condition, including rickets. Because she couldn't speak, Isabelle was given intensive skilled treatment by a speech therapist. She went through all the usual stages of language development at a very rapid rate, covering in two years, stages that normally take six, e.g. after two months of treatment she was speaking in sentences, after nine months she was reading and writing and, by the age of eight and a half (and at the later follow-up at age fourteen), she was considered normal. Isabelle's early experience of non-verbal communication with her mother was probably very important in laying the base for language acquisition.

Anna was also an illegitimate child who was confined to an attic, this time alone. When discovered at the age of six, she could not walk, talk, or do anything that demonstrated intelligence. Anna did not learn to speak, but did learn to look after her personal needs, to walk, to follow simple instructions and to recognise people and things. She died four and a half years after her discovery. Unfortunately, we cannot assess which of several factors was more important in determining the poorer outcome for Anna – her isolation was more extreme than Isabelle's, she didn't receive such skilled treatment, her physical condition was poorer and there is a possibility that she was more damaged initially.

Kiluchova (1972, 1976) studied twin boys whose mother died at their birth. They had a normal institutional upbringing until the age of eighteen months when they were taken by their father and psychopathic stepmother who imprisoned them in a small room (the father was dominated by the stepmother and worked away from home a lot, so did little to help the twins). They had few furnishings or play things and were frequently beaten. When they were discovered at the age of seven, they had rickets, could not walk or speak, did not understand the meaning of pictures and had a measured mental age of about three. The parents' defence at their trial was that they had done their best for the twins who had been defective from the beginning. The psychologists refuted this by pointing out that the twins were frightened by many common experiences and objects which they had clearly never encountered before – well-cared for children, however retarded, would not be **frightened** by such things because they would be familiar with them (e.g. the twins were horrified by a TV set and by traffic in the street). The twins were given skilled educational treatment and were placed in a secure foster home. By the age of eleven (and at the later follow-up at age fourteen), they were considered to be intellectually, socially and emotionally normal. In assessing the implications of this study, it is important to remember that the twins spent the first eighteen months of their life in a nutritionally normal environment (i.e. during the 'critical period' for brain growth). It is likely that the bases for perceptual and linguistic development were laid down during this period. The twins' social experience with each other was probably also very important in helping to account for the surprisingly good outcome.

Tizard *et al.* (1972) carried out a number of studies on the development of young children in residential nurseries run by Dr Barnardo's Society, the Church of England Children's Society and the National Children's Home. She makes the point that institutions have improved enormously since the 1940s – they are well equipped and staffed, and an attempt is made to provide the children with plenty of books, toys, etc., and outside experiences. In a study of eleven different institutions, Tizard *et al.* found that all of the environments were good enough to promote at least average intellectual and language development but that, beyond this, level of development of language comprehension was related to the quality of staff talk, in particular the amount of **informative** talk. A high proportion of informative talk from staff to children was found in those nurseries where there was high staff autonomy (where individual members of staff had the power to make many day-to-day decisions on their own initiative) and where staff members were generally kept with the same group of children rather than being switched around. Although the 'verbal environments' provided were often very good, the institutions still lacked two things which Bowlby considered crucial for mental health – close attachments to staff were discouraged and there was no long-term continuity of care by a particular person. By the age of four and a half, the children had on average been cared for by fifty different nurses for at least a week. The children reacted to this emotional deprivation in one of two ways: some appeared emotionally detached and uninterested in either strange or familiar adults; others were very attention seeking and tried to attach themselves to any adult who showed interest, yet were apparently unconcerned at the disappearance of this adult. This is just the kind of behaviour about which Bowlby, Goldfarb and others had warned and which they thought would be permanent. In the past, this made the authorities reluctant to recommend such children for adoption. Tizard *et al.* followed the progress of twenty-four children who were adopted at the age of three plus (i.e. after Bowlby's 'critical period' for bond formation) and found that, by the age of four and a half, twenty of these children were considered by their adoptive mothers to have formed a deep attachment to them and indeed to be unusually affectionate. They also showed no more behaviour problems than a contrast group of children growing up in their own families. These findings are even more encouraging when we take into account the fact that many of these children were initially 'adoption rejects' whose placement was delayed because there was a family history of mental illness or mental retardation.

Schaffer (1958, 1965, 1966) identified two 'post-hospitalisation syndromes', each associated with a particular age group. The 'over-dependent' syndrome involves excessive crying, clinging, fear of strangers, etc. and is characteristic of children over the age of seven months who are old enough to know and miss their mothers as individuals. This lasts from a few days to a few months after leaving hospital. The 'global syndrome' involves extreme preoccupation with the environment (scanning the surroundings without seeming to attend to any particular thing) and is characteristic of younger babies who perhaps have not yet fully differentiated themselves from their environment – Schaffer considers that perceptual monotony in hospitals (being kept in one position with the same view) is an essential precondition of the development of the 'global syndrome' which normally only lasts for a day or two after leaving hospital. In another study, Schaffer demonstrated that there was less depression of DQ (Developmental Quotient) in hospital in babies who were active and who therefore provided themselves with more stimulation, either directly or indirectly (as a result of crying and being picked up more). Disturbance of sleeping and feeding patterns is common in all age groups and may have an emotional component, even in very young babies.

Douglas (1975) studied children who had experienced early or repeated admission to hospital. There was a relationship between such admissions and ratings in adolescence for 'troublesomeness', 'poor reading', 'delinquency' and 'unstable job pattern'. Douglas concludes that the "evidence.... though highly suggestive, does not establish the existence of a causal relationship between early hospital admissions and later behaviour. For that an experimental study would be required." Yet he also shows that children hospitalised in the early years are more likely to return to hospital, have persisting physical disability, be boys, from large families, and have manual-worker parents who take little interest in their schooling.

One particularly important question for health professionals to consider is, "What effect might illness and hospitalisation have on the development of the child?" Whilst it is acknowledged that the quality of a child's early experience is undoubtedly important in his/her development, recent research indicates that children are more resilient than the studies of the 1950s and 1960s suggest. It is the entire experience of childhood which is important, rather than simply attachment and the formation of bonds. Deprivation and disadvantage at one age can be overcome, or at least lessened, by later experience. For the child who is hospitalised through illness, it is essential that he/she is provided with a stimulating environment, with things to look at and toys to play with, and that satisfying and close relationships are developed and maintained.

Useful Reading

Bradley, B.S., (1989). *Visions of Infancy*, Polity Press
Burn, R.B., (1986). *Child Development: A Text for Caring Professionals*, Croom Helm
Clarke, A.M. & Clarke, A.D.B., (1976). *Early Experience – Myth and Evidence*, Open Books
Dawkins, (1966). *The Selfish Gene*, Oxford University Press
Mussen, P.H. *et al.*, (1980). *Essentials of Child Development and Personality*, Harper Row
Rutter, M., (1975). *Maternal Deprivation Reassessed*, Penguin
Slater, A. & Brenner, G. (eds.), (1989). *Infant Development*, LEA
Tomlinson, P., (1981). *Interactive Educational Psychology*, McGraw Hill

Chapter 4
Understanding children's experience of illness and hospitalisation

In communicating with children about illness and health, it is essential to determine their powers of comprehension. Children are not miniature adults; hence their understanding and interpretation of the meaning of illness and hospitalisation will differ from that of an adult.

Piaget (1896 – 1980) concluded from his research findings that children do, in fact, think in radically different ways. Piaget was concerned with the cognitive processes involved in development and attempted to trace the development of logical thinking from infancy to adolescence. He sees the child as having cognitive structures or **schema** which adapt to changes in the environment. Two mechanisms are involved in adaption: **assimilation** and **accommodation**. Assimilation refers to the incorporation of new environmental events into existing structures. In other words, it implies reacting to a situation in terms of existing schema. For example, an infant has an innate capacity or mechanism allowing him/her to suck for milk. This sucking scheme is extended and assimilation said to occur when the infant uses this mechanism to suck also his/her fingers, blanket or toys. Accommodation refers to changing those cognitive structures or schema in order to cope with a new problem. This is likely to occur when the child meets something which is novel and which cannot be assimilated into existing schemes. For example, a child with a scheme for coping with a hinged box might, initially, have difficulty with a match box because it opens in a very different way.

According to Piaget, the child goes through four major stages of intellectual development where qualitative changes occur. Piaget does not attach absolute ages to these stages; what is important is the sequence of stages rather than the age at which each stage is attained. In other words, children develop through these stages in a particular order, but some are slower whilst others are quicker to reach them. However, children develop much earlier now and so it is important to note that Piaget's approximate ages relating to each of the stages is outdated. Nevertheless, in the case of the hospitalised child, it is critical that cognitive developmental stages or processes are recognised alongside physical development if the child is to receive total care where both physical and psychological needs are met.

Piaget refers to the first stage of cognitive development as the **sensorimotor period**. He subdivides this stage into a further six stages that cover cognitive development from birth to about 18 months to two years of age. In the first of these six stages, the child's actions are innate, based upon reflexes not thoughts, and include sucking, grasping and eye-movements. In stage two, at about one to four months, the child's actions are based upon vision. In stage three, at the age of four to eight months, the child is able to co-ordinate actions. At stage four (8–12 months), the child becomes more goal directed. His/her cognitive development is enhanced by increasing motor skills and by language acquisition. At stage five, the child is able to use trial-and-error behaviour to solve problems. He/she differentiates self from object and increases his/her exploration of how objects function. When the child has reached the sixth stage of cognitive development, he/she is primed for the next major stage. The child now has the ability to form a mental picture of his/her external body and can deliberately use trial and error as a means of solving problems.

During the sensorimotor stage of cognitive development, (particularly the later stages), it should be recognised, in a care situation, that the child can differentiate between parents and strangers; therefore, 'stranger' anxiety may be a problem for the hospitalised child. Nursing care at this stage needs to be geared towards ensuring parental contact is maintained (keeping in mind long-term ill effects which may occur through early separation of the child from its parents). Nursing procedure, equipment and treatment should be explained to the child in simple terms in order to alleviate anxiety and distress.

Piaget refers to the second stage of cognitive development as the **preoperational period** which, according to Piaget, occurs from two to seven years of age. Initially, at this stage, the child forms memories, imitates behaviour and mixes fantasy and reality. The child's symbolic behaviour increases at the ages of two to four years. At four to seven years, the child uses intuitive thought and begins to think more in language than in symbols alone. During this stage, the child can make physical comparisons but not mental ones. Also at this stage, the child is egocentric (self-centred in thought); he/she sees the world existing solely for his/her own benefit. The child is only able to retain one aspect of a situation in his/her mind at any one time. The child attempts logical thinking but lacks perspective; therefore, false logic and inconsistent thinking results. In the preoperational period, the child will judge things as they look. As the child nears the end of this cognitive developmental stage, he/she becomes aware of cause-and-effect relationships.

This preoperational period of cognitive development requires careful consideration when caring for the hospitalised child. It needs to be borne in mind that the child is egocentric and therefore is unable to see the point of view of others and may feel that hospitalisation and treatment is a form of punishment. The child at this stage is deeply concerned with consequences for themselves. They do not understand internal body structures so procedures and treatments need to be explained in simple terms. Children aged two to seven years do not understand the word 'test' for example, and will be confused by its use (children over seven years understand the word 'test' as something they will pass or fail and are equally confused). The word 'cut' will imply pain to a very young child and the word 'fix' will suggest something is broken. Therefore, to ensure that less anxiety, fear and stress is suffered by the sick or disabled child, the language of the carer must be very carefully chosen. School-aged children can relate to drawings, models and pictures and these may be used to show the consequences of treatment, perhaps by applying plaster casts or bandages to a doll, then removing them to demonstrate to the child that the doll is not harmed by such procedures and, therefore, the child has nothing to fear. Similarly, models of internal body structures can be used to reassure the child.

This second stage, coupled with the third stage referred to as the **concrete operational period**, from seven to eleven years of age, is where Piaget showed most concern. He conducted numerous experiments to highlight the differences in intellectual ability between these two stages of cognitive development. The concrete operational period is characterised by the child's development of conservation. Piaget's experiments show that in the preoperational period, the child shown liquid placed into different-shaped glasses will equate the amount of liquid with the size of the glass, and that the child at this stage has difficulty understanding conservation. The child in the concrete operational stage is able to keep more than one aspect of a situation or object in mind at the same time and is able to acknowledge that situations are reversible. Therefore, the child at this stage will overcome conservation problems. Piaget's experiments show that this is true of conservation of numbers, space and measurement. The child also becomes less egocentric at this stage. However, he/she has still not reached adult thought and still has difficulty in dealing with causal relationships. It is vital that the carer is able to recognise the differences between the cognitive ability of children in the preoperational and that of children in the concrete operational stage of cognitive development to ensure that care procedures are directed accordingly, as the child's concept and response to illness, treatment and hospitalisation will be greatly affected by the level of cognition he/she has reached.

The final stage of cognitive development, the formal operational stage occurs from eleven to sixteen years of age. According to Piaget, this is when the child develops a form of thinking that is organised, systematic and logical. The child begins to think of things that cannot be seen, for example philosophy or religion. The child can link variables to formulate hypotheses and can relate his/her own thought to others and cope with causal relationships. This advancement in cognitive development needs to be sensitively borne in mind by the carer in a health care setting.

Piaget's attempt to examine the cognitive development of children seems to be a very ambitious and creative theory which has been extensively applied, particularly in the area of education, and, more recently, in the health profession. Nevertheless, several criticisms can be levelled at the theory and a number of studies have questioned the psychological validity of his approach.

First, Piaget's initial work, using his own three children, presents methodological problems. For instance, the sample was small and restricted, and the family influences and similarities would bias the outcome of results. Second, the 'verbal clinical method' (interview) is open to debate; leading questions may have been put to the child, the effects of the interviewer and the child upon each other may have introduced an additional element of bias, and the interpretation of the child's responses may be misleading. This latter point links to the meaning and use of language and also to the idea that any inadequate answer by the child may be because of a limited vocabulary rather than any limitations in thought or cognitive development. The question has to be asked: is thought adequately reflected through language? Third, Piaget claims that young children fail conservation tasks because of a lack of understanding due to not having reached the concrete operational stage. However, Donaldson and McGarrigle (1974) suggest linguistic reasons instead, that is, a failure to understand the meaning of the question. There is also the possibility of non-linguistic reasons why children fail conservation tasks, for example a child may be distracted and therefore not listen to the instructions relating to the task. Bryant (1971) suggests the possibility that a child may have a limited memory capacity, so tasks are not correctly completed because the child cannot remember all of the instructions upon which the task is based. Fourth, Piaget claimed that children are egocentric until between the ages of around seven to eleven years (the concrete operational period), but Hughes and Donaldson (1983) found that, if the task is explained carefully and makes sense to the child, children as young as three and four years of age can see things from another person's point of view.

Illness in childhood places the child immediately into a stressful situation for which he/she may or may not have the emotional, behavioural or cognitive abilities to cope. For example, the very young child in the sensorimotor stage and perhaps the preoperational stage does not have a very good understanding of cause-and-effect relationships; hence he/she may be confused about pain, treatment, admission to hospital and why he/she has become sick. In fact, the child may see the illness as some kind of punishment. For instance, Schowalter (1970) reviewed children's reactions to illness and concluded that a child between the ages of three and six years may consider illness as a form of retribution for bad thoughts or actions. This may lead the child to feel guilty or inferior and to develop a self-concept that tells them they are different and that there is something wrong with them. For this reason, it is important that the health professional has some understanding of what stage (**not age**) the child might be at and how the child may perceive illness, health and the sick role.

Sudden admission to hospital can cause the child a great deal of distress so, where possible, some kind of preparatory programme can be worked out, for example, visits to hospital prior to admission and playing games similar to likely hospital experiences. This will allow the child the opportunity to assimilate and accommodate the potential experiences. Play in early childhood is taken to reveal a child's preoccupations. Play therapy is based on the notion that these preoccupations can be acted out. It is important then that the young child is provided with concrete materials, such as objects and toys. Children need concrete examples in order to understand their illness and treatment. In this sense, it may be useful to adopt Plank's (1971) pioneering use of outline diagrams of the child's body on which can be drawn the faulty organs whilst explanations can be given about what the doctors are going to do. Petrillo *et al.* (1972) showed that using rag dolls on which stitches could be sewn or catheters and tubes attached was a productive way of explaining procedures to children. It is the case that children under seven years of age are more egocentric, cannot take into account the perspective of others and, therefore, may have an inappropriate perception of their illness. Thus, it is important at this stage to encourage children to interact with their peers in order to facilitate a more socialised view of the world and, hopefully, a more realistic and perhaps less threatening view of their illness. Bearison (1982) argued that it is not possible to explain a child's cognitive development purely in terms of their individual encounters with the environment and demonstrated how children learn more easily and readily when working together rather than alone.

Niven (1989) remarks that many of our ideas about illness are wrong because we either have incorrect information or not all of the available information. This is the case for adults as well as children. Children may also make mistakes because they have a different perspective of the world and their environment. However, it is important not to assume that children of particular ages cannot understand details concerning illness and health because they have not yet developed the cognitive ability. Niven (1986) found that children as young as five and six years of age were quite sophisticated with their answers to questions about illness. For instance, when asked how you catch a cold, many children claimed "from germs", although a few remarked that it was from stopping in the bath too long. The point needs to be raised, however, that a number of adults would probably give the same response.

Bibace and Walsh (1979), on the basis of their interviews about illness and health with 180 children aged three to eight years of age concluded that information given to the child must be pitched at his/her level of cognitive ability. Assessing cognitive ability is difficult because it comprises several personhood features that are unobservable and can only be inferred. Ward-Platt (1986) remarks that a child's comprehension is far in advance of their ability to communicate and so a child is likely to understand explanations about illness and treatment but be unable to be articulate about his/her own perceptions. This begs the question of what is the relationship between language and thought? The following section focuses upon language development and its relationship with the development of thinking.

Useful Reading

Bibace, R. & Walsh, M.E., (1979). Developmental stages in children's conception of illness. In Stone, G.C. *et al.*(eds.) *Health Psychology*, Jossey Bass

Branthwaite, A. & Rogers, D., (1985). *Children Growing Up*, Open University Press

Donaldson, M., (1978). *Children's Minds*, Fontana

Niven, N., (1989). *Health Psychology*, Churchill Livingstone

Parmelee, A.H., (1986). Children's illnesses: their beneficial effects on behavioural development. *Child Development*, **57**, 1–10

Ward-Platt, M., (1989). Personal communication

Chapter 5
The development of language and the relationship between language and thought

Broca (1861) was concerned with the neurological basis of language and published his findings from having studied the brain of a patient who had suffered from a form of aphasia (disruption of speech). Each half of the brain, the right and left hemispheres, are dominant for several functions. The left side is usually dominant for language. Any destruction or damage to the frontal lobe in the left hemisphere can leave speech slow and hesitant and result in badly produced sounds and sometimes defective writing. However, the patient's comprehension of spoken and written language may be excellent. What is also interesting is that a person may produce defective speech but he/she usually sings very well. It is thought that the neurological basis for the production of musical sounds lies in the right hemisphere of the brain. In contrast to Broca's area in the frontal lobe, Wernicke (1874) identified a major speech area which could be located in the temporal lobe. The speech of Wernicke's aphasic is quite different from that of the Broca type. The patient may speak very rapidly, well articulated and melodically. He/she experiences difficulty, however, in using the correct or appropriate words and may even use non-existent words. There are other areas of the brain involved in language function, damage to which may lead to other distinctive language disorders, such as loss of the ability to understand written language, loss of the ability to comprehend spoken language, loss of the ability to write correct language or loss of the ability to carry out movements on the basis of a verbal command even though the command has been understood.

Extensive damage to any of the important language areas in adulthood, generally results in permanent damage. In children, however, even excessive damage to the left hemisphere, before the age or around eight to nine years can be overcome; the child is usually able to recover and acquire language in a period of time ranging from several months to three years. The main reason for this recovery or late acquisition is that the right hemisphere has the potential to become the centre for language. This process is not fully understood; nevertheless, future knowledge may lead to more effective forms of treatment and therapy for older patients who find recovery almost impossible.

The central question is, "How do children acquire language?" Current knowledge places emphasis upon competence: some theorists suggest linguistic competence is necessary and others argue that a child requires communicative competence.

Behaviourist theories of language acquisition depend upon the notions of imitation and reinforcement. Language behaviour is seen to be like any other form of behaviour, and the acquisition of it can be explained in terms of a collection of habits, associations and connections between stimuli and responses. Language is learned, shaped and conditioned by adults through reinforcement and imitation of speech. The problem for the behaviourists, however, is that they cannot account for the novel and creative utterances a child makes. For example, the child is unlikely to have heard the word 'sheeps' or 'sheepses'; it is more probable that the child has constructed these words him/herself by over generalising grammatical rules. This emphasises the point that a child is active rather than passive, explores the world and words as opposed to being simply a recipient of what the environment has to offer.

Chomsky (1967) criticised the early simplistic behaviour views by pointing out that many of the child's early utterances are novel combinations which he/she will never have heard modelled by the parents. In their innatist theories, they argued that persons must have an innate **language acquisition device (LAD)** because the child's acquisition of language is so rapid and effective, it could not possibly be based upon the 'poor' samples of language heard by the child, that is, the fast, incomplete and sometimes mumbled language of adult conversation. Chomsky also proposed that language is localised in the brain, which suggests that persons have evolved a specific language capacity, and that persons are the only species to acquire language.

These assumptions made by Chomsky, however, have since been cast in doubt. There is now ample evidence that, when speaking to children, adults produce short, clear and slowly paced utterances. It is now thought that other species, such as dolphins, have a complex language of their own, and, in America, chimpanzees have been taught sign language used by the deaf. There is no evidence to support the hypothesis of any innate specifically linguistic ability, although the possession of a large complex brain is probably important in that it allows us to develop language among other complex cognitive skills. However, there does seem to be some maturational base and possibly a sensitive period for language learning. The case of **Genie** illustrates this.

Genie was nearly fourteen years old before hearing languages; her father was intolerant of noise and punished Genie, whom he believed to be mentally retarded when she vocalised at all. Genie's mother was nearly blind and, to placate the father, spoke very softly, probably inaudibly to the child. Eventually, the mother ran away with Genie and she was admitted to hospital. Genie was still able to learn to speak, although, in Brown's (1977) report, she was still a long way from normal competence. Normally, in right-handed people, the left side of the brain is dominant in language comprehension and production. This can be tested by feeding different messages to each ear – normally the right ear (i.e. left brain) will show better reception of verbal content and the left ear (right brain) will show better reception of music and other non-verbal sounds. Genie was right-handed but her dichotic listening performance showed an extreme left-ear advantage which points to right-hemisphere dominance for language – unusual in a right-handed person.

Genie also showed a normal left-ear advantage for non-verbal sounds, showing that hers was not just a rare case of reversed dominance. It seems that areas of Genie's brain which would normally be available for language functions had become specialised for other purposes and were no longer available for language. The fact that Genie's environment and developmental possibilities had been so restricted may explain why she was able to acquire language at such a late age. In a more demanding environment, all of her brain may have been taken over by other functions and she may have completely lost the capacity for normal language development. Lenneberg (1967, 1969) has cited cases of deaf children who never developed normal language because adequate hearing aids were made available too late. It seems that though we have neutral structures that can be used for specific language functions, these can be switched to other functions if the environment doesn't keep them on a linguistic track.

Similarly, innatist approaches to language development have been cast in doubt and superseded by cognitive approaches. Cognitive theorists emphasise the dependence of language on prior cognitive achievements. Cromer (1976) believes that thoughts, intentions and meanings are cognitions which underpin language and that language development is dependent upon these cognitions. The child is seen to map language on to his/her non-verbal concepts by listening to language in contexts which provide additional cues to meaning. The representation in play of concepts is a further indication that thought precedes language development. In simple terms, the child has to have something to say before he/she can express it and the child has to mean something when he/she speaks.

Prior to considering the social context and its influence upon language, it is useful to cite the case of **John** who appeared to have developed an ability for language but found difficulty in communicating.

John was referred for special help at the age of three years three months because of his failure to speak to anyone other than his parents (he didn't even speak to his grandmother with whom he had a close attachment). The parents stated that a worrying symptom in babyhood was a total lack of interest in playful preverbal communication – they could not recall his ever having responded to peek-a-boo or pat-a-cake, nor ever having pointed or waved bye-bye. They became concerned about his language development and, in an effort to encourage this, repeatedly talked to him about books and objects. Gradually John began to produce phrases and sentences similar to the ones the parents had modelled (these were rarely direct imitations – he generated novel combinations from the start). If the toy that was eliciting the language, was removed John stopped speaking and might be completely silent for as long as one or two hours or until his parents introduced another of the 'special' toys which had acted as a stimulus for language. It seems, therefore, that John's language both developed and was used in symbolic play situations. It rarely appeared in the more typical communicative ways that are characteristic of young children's initial language development, such as requests to meet needs ("more apple"), gain attention ("hello", "look") or assert independence ("me do it"). However, once John's language was well developed in play routines, he began to use it to describe real events – a reversal of the usual direction of development. It appeared that he had learned to understand the sensorimotor world and had ultimately combined this knowledge with the language he had learned in game-like sequences with his parents. From his continuing failure to understand such simple communications as pointing and his failure to respond directly to communication from his parents, John's language must be regarded as 'non-communicative'. Such language is a common feature of young autistic children but these children rarely display the range of well-formulated, age-appropriate utterances that John could produce.

More recently, psychologists have stressed the social context as a precursor to language. Indeed, at an early stage, the child can direct his/her parent's attention to something in the environment simply by focusing his/her gaze upon that something. Subsequently, grasping movements can be made towards the object and, later still, a gesture towards or pointing to it will indicate some form of communicative language. Bruner suggests that it is through this manipulation of his/her social environment that the child is laying the foundations for communicative competence.

The notion of competence is a difficult one and is to be distinguished from performance. Performance is there to be observed and can be measured, unlike competence which is not directly observable and can only be inferred. The question arises, "Is competence reflected in performance?" If linguistic competence can be measured through speech performance, how is cognitive competence to be assessed? This brings us full circle to the complex relationship that exists between thought and language. Is the development of thought prior to and necessary for the development of language (as advocated by Piaget) or is language necessary for thought (as proposed by the behaviourists)?

Vygotsky (1937) took an interactive position, contending that language and thought originate as independent activities which ultimately form a reciprocal relationship. In other words, neither language nor thought is dependent upon the other for its existence. Initially, thought is without speech and speech is without thought. Subsequently, speech becomes rational and thought becomes verbal, and, finally, language is used for social communication and thought is used for internalised speech. In effect, Vygotsky suggested that, ultimately, language has two functions: external communication and the internal manipulation of one's own thoughts. However, is the language that we communicate with socially the same kind of language that we use for thinking? For example, why is it sometimes difficult for us to put into words what we are thinking? As Cohen (1983) remarks, language suitable for communication may not necessarily be suitable for thought. Conversely, language easily internalised is not necessarily communicated with the same degree of ease. So, how adequately does language reflect thought? Can we say that a person is mentally ill and has thought disorder (a typical 'symptom' of someone classified as schizophrenic) simply because speech is disordered?

Cohen (1983) comments that the controversies between language and thought arise because there is little consensus of opinion as to what constitutes thinking and what is to count as language. She suggests a more productive approach to the issue would be to determine how effective thought can be in the absence of language and how well disabled thinkers can master a language. Indeed, this approach may prove useful in a practical sense, as long as it is borne in mind that determining what is meant by effective thought and disabled thinking rests upon inference and subjective judgements.

Whatever the controversies and complexities, language and thought are central to effective communication between the health professional and patient. It is essential in order to facilitate individualised care of the person that the health professional is aware that a person may not be verbalising what he/she is thinking, may be unable to express his/her thoughts, may hear words but not understand them or that the non-verbal communication may not match what they are saying. In effect, health professionals ought to be highly skilled in communication, having an in-depth knowledge of how best to exchange information, how to listen, to ask questions, to read non-verbal cues, and to have an understanding of the different meanings of language, the influence of the social context and the complexities of the relationship between language and thought.

An important area where the relationship between language and thought is central, relates to introspection, Rogerian therapy and Freudian psychoanalysis. **Psychoanalysis** is a form of treatment/therapy which uses hypnosis, dream analysis and free association in order to assess the unconscious. Previous experiences and feelings are revealed by the patient/client who is at liberty to disclose anything which comes into his/her mind. The therapist interprets this information and attaches meaning to it. So, the patient/client is revealing the contents of his/her unconscious mind through language. The problem arises, however, if some ideas have been repressed in the unconscious mind. Is any meaning lost when they are somehow transferred to the conscious mind and is additional significance lost when ideas, now in the conscious or even subconscious mind, are converted into a form suitable for communication? Further, are repressed ideas accurately stored in memory and retrieved from memory? Does the recall of experiences from memory distort their eventual expression in language? Is there any relationship between the unconscious mind and memory; indeed, are they distinct or one and the same thing?

Rogerian therapy relies upon listening to the person's reflection upon his/her own past experiences. The therapist ought not to impose any values or judgements or make any kind of interpretation; simply listen and reflect back to the person what he/she has just said. Reflecting upon one's own experience involves **introspection**. Introspection implies the direct observation of one's own mental processes, but this notion of us having private access to our own inner states is controversial. Kant claimed that an individual cannot reason and, at the same time, observe that reasoning. Further, the attempt to give a verbal report whilst observing and reasoning about one's own inner thoughts can lead to an inaccurate account of those mental processes. De Groot (1965) puts this quite succinctly:

> "the added instruction to think aloud necessarily influences the thought processes to some degree ... and concentrated thinking on the problem itself must somehow hamper its reporting ... quite often thoughts move so quickly that the spoken word cannot keep up with them. The individual is then forced to skip steps

> or to deliberately slow down his/her thinking (if possible) which thereby disturbs the thought processes."

Valentine (1982) remarks that, if a person delays their verbal message (which individuals invariably do), then they may forget what actually happened and, therefore, memory errors creep in. For example, if a patient delays consulting the GP or delays informing the nurse of certain experiences, like pain, then it is likely that some of the information will be forgotten. Also, when a person reflects back, he/she may view certain experiences, signs or symptoms as less significant and, therefore, report them with a different emphasis and meaning.

Discussion Points

1. Do we acquire language before thought or thought before language?

2. When you think, what do you think in – words, pictures or something else we find difficult to describe?

3. Suppose someone is born blind, deaf and dumb. How then does such an individual learn to think, learn language and learn to communicate?

4. How can the health professional help the stroke patient to adapt to his/her loss of linguistic or cognitive competence?

Useful Reading

Clark, H.H. & Clark, E.V., (1977). *Psychology and Language*, Harcourt, Brace & Jovanovch
Cohen, G., (1983). *The Psychology of Cognition*, Academic Press
Donaldson, M., (1978). *Children's Minds*, Fontana
Elliot, A., (1981). *Child Language*, Cambridge University Press
Fletcher, P. & Garman, M., (1986). *Language Acquisition: Studies in First Language Development*, Cambridge University Press
Greene, J., (1975). *Thinking and Language*, Methuen
Lloyd, A. & Mayes, P., (1984). *Introduction to Psychology*, Fontana
Valentine, E., (1982). *Conceptual Issues in Psychology*, Allen & Unwin

Section 3

INDIVIDUAL DIFFERENCES

Individual differences which distinguish one person from another result from an interaction between genetic/physiological characteristics and predispositions and active experience within a social context. In effect, persons are unique, possess idiosyncratic physiological, psychological and social features which, in turn, influence how he/she perceives, reacts and copes with life's experiences, including illness.

The intention of this next section is to focus selectively on three particular psychological aspects which contribute to our being individually different, namely personality, perception and intelligence.

Chapter 6
Personality and its influence upon our behaviour and experience of illness

What is personality: a single property of the individual, a cluster of traits or the whole person? Are we born with our personality or do we develop it? Personality is a broad term that includes how people think, feel and behave. Barnouw defines personality as "the more or less enduring organisation of forces within the individual associated with a complex of fairly consistent attitudes, values and models of perception which account, in part, for the individual's consistency of behaviour." However, an entirely satisfactory and universally acceptable definition of personality is hard to come by because the word means different things to different people depending upon their theoretical assumptions. There are many schools of thought which adopt radically different perspectives, but one of the ways to look at personality theory is to classify the theories on the basis of how far they support either a hereditary (nature) view or an environmental (nurture) view. The nature/nurture debate is central to many of the opposing theories and explanations of different psychological concepts. The dichotomy implies that we are either born with something, like our personality, intelligence or motivation, or we acquire and develop these features through experience in the environment.

Most people probably wonder why they are who they are, why it is that they are and why they behave as they do. Perhaps an understanding of personality theory can explain some of these questions. Similarly, it is important for a health professional to have some understanding of his/her own personality and some understanding of a patient's personality. Why is it that some patients perceive, react and cope with their illness in an aggressive manner whilst others are subdued but equally anxious? Why are some patients demanding and others independent and why do some patients admit to their fear and anxiety whilst others deny it and pretend they can cope?

Some theorists propose that personality is biologically based. Sheldon (1951) proposed that there is some kind of association between body type and temperament. His research involved analysing 4000 photographs of male nude college students. He identified three main dimensions of body build which, he claimed, could be associated with the relative influence of three primitive embryonic layers. A follow-up study using thirty-three individuals (eleven from each of the three main types) revealed significant correlations between these types and certain personality traits.

The **endomorph** was described as soft and round with an overdeveloped viscera. The temperament is relaxed, sociable, affectionate and loves comfort. The **mesomorph** was described as muscular with ample bone and connective tissue. The personality is characterised as energetic, noisy, aggressive, assertive, concerned with the present and meets problems with action. The **ectomorph** was described as linear, fragile, narrow-shouldered, delicate body and flat-chested (most men are!). This type employs excessive restraint, an inhibition of action, tends to withdraw from the social contact, is fearful, introverted and artistic.

Perhaps there is some 'commonsense' support for this view of personality, for example, we make value judgements about people on the basis of their physical appearance. We hold stereotyped ideas that fat people are lazy and jolly and have expectations that a 'he-man' type ought not to have a feminine voice. However, there is much to indicate that these associations between physique and personality are spurious. What about the individual endomorph who decides to diet; with weight loss does he/she suddenly become an ectomorph?

Sheldon's research was carried out on a sample of the male population and yet he applied these same types to females. This extension of his findings has to be questioned, particularly since, biologically, the sexes are quite different. For instance, can only flat-chested women be classified as ectomorph? This would certainly exclude almost half the population from being of this particular type.

Eysenck (1958, 1972) contends that the basis of an individual's personality can be found in his/her inherited physiological make-up. Eysenck places emphasis upon the basic neural structures in the brain and the central nervous system, but recognises also that experience is required for personality to develop.

Eysenck uses three major dimensions in order to account for behaviour: the **extrovert/introvert** scale, the **neuroticism/stability** scale and **psychotic/normal** scale. He believes that these three basic dimensions are the relatively simple starting points for personality. He argues that personality becomes more diverse and individualised in terms of actual behaviour as individuals experience the interaction of their basic types with the realities of everyday life experience.

Eysenck developed his theory of personality after his involvement with, and study of, 700 neurotic soldiers during World War II. He established the extrovert/introvert and neurotic/stable scales on the basis of a factor analysis carried out on thirty-nine items of personal data pertaining to the soldiers. These dimensions were supported by further extensive research. In a later investigation with psychiatric patients, he established the third dimension, unrelated to the first two, referred to as the psychotic/normal scale. It is important to emphasise, however, that most of Eysenck's work and theory has focused upon the extroversion and neuroticism dimensions.

The following descriptions of the different types proposed by Eysenck relate to extreme ends of the dimensions or continuums, and so it is crucial to keep in mind that few individuals would fit them completely. The majority of people fall somewhere between; more specifically, most people are neither strongly extroverted nor strongly introverted, nor strongly neurotic. The typical extrovert is sociable, outward going, prefering people to objects, generally impulsive, active, optimistic, sometimes aggressive and has feelings which are not necessarily well controlled. The typical introvert is shy, withdrawn, content to be alone, introspective, prefers a planned and well-ordered mode of life, places value upon ethical standards and keeps his/her feelings under tight control.

The extroversion/introversion dimension is based upon specific physiological claims concerning the brain and the central nervous system which are responsible for controlling the level of arousal. Eysenck proposed that extroverts are physiologically under-roused and seek to correct this imbalance by searching out stimulation and new experiences. Conversely, introverts are held to be physiologically over-roused and therefore, attempt to reduce this level of arousal by avoiding extra stimulation from the outside world.

Much research has been carried out describing how these differences between introverts and extroverts affect behaviour, tolerance of pain, sensory deprivation, drug taking and lifestyle in old age.

Eysenck considers that extroverts have nervous systems in which conditioned behavioural responses are only formed slowly and weakly. In other words, those individuals who are physiologically under-aroused or whose nervous system is inhibited are resistant to conditioning. In effect, extroverts are under-socialised and, according to Eysenck, more likely to become criminals and psychopaths. Conversely, introverts are held to have easily aroused nervous systems with a strong and rapid build up of excitation which favours strong and rapid conditioning; hence introverts are over-socialised, more likely to feel guilty, anxious and over-conscientious.

Pain in childbirth has been studied and it was found that introverts feel pain sooner and more intensely, complained less and remembered their pain more vividly than extroverts. Extroverts are more tolerant of pain but communicate it more freely because of a greater readiness to brave the possibility of social disapproval for complaining.

Depressants, like alcohol, have been found to make introverts less aroused and, therefore, behave more like extroverts. In other words, the normally high internal level of physiological arousal is depressed by the alcohol and places the introvert in a position of having to seek external stimulation. In contrast, stimulants, like caffeine, have been claimed to have the effect of making extroverts behave more like introverts because their usually low level of internal physiological arousal has been stimulated and, therefore, they require less stimulation from the external world.

Work on personality and life style in old age has found that introversion increases with age. This implies that as people get older they become more preoccupied with themselves, their thoughts, feelings and memories and less concerned with the outside world and other people. This links to the **disengagement theory** that has been put forward to explain such a change. It claims that there is decreased concern for social interaction and an increased satisfaction with one's own world of memories and immediate surroundings. This will be discussed in more detail in a later section. However, it is important to point out that, with *some* elderly people, this kind of reaction may be forced upon them through undesired physical and social changes, for instance, illness, disability, bereavement, loss of occupational role.

The typical neurotic tends to over-worry, is touchy, anxiety prone, excitable, moody and frequently depressed. He/she may suffer from various psychosomatic disorders. Eysenck links neuroticism to the limbic system and the autonomic nervous system (ANS). The ANS governs the expression of emotions, including fear, and controls the heart rate, respiratory rate, gut activity etc. In neurotics, the ANS is highly responsive to stimulation and, therefore, emotional reactions frequently occur.

On the basis of his theory Eysenck developed various questionnaires which, he claims, can measure individual scores on each of the three dimensions. The most commonly used one is the Eysenck Personality Inventory (EPI). Wilson-Barnett (1976) used a version of the EPI on 202 patients and found that neuroticism was closely related to levels of anxiety and depression suffered by patients in a hospital environment. A high N score does not mean that the person is neurotic, but merely at greater risk. The more anxiety prone someone is, the more likely they are to develop an actual neurosis as a form of personality disorder. Mathews and Ridgeway (1981) used the EPI and found that a high score on the neuroticism dimension may mean an individual will have delayed or complicated recovery from surgery.

The dimension of psychoticism is the most recent addition to Eysenck's description of personality. High scorers on this scale are solitary, not caring for people, often troublesome, not fitting in anywhere, may be cruel and inhumane, lacking in feeling and empathy and altogether insensitive, hostile to others, having a liking for odd and unusual things and a disregard for danger. Whereas the distribution in the population of extroversion and neuroticism is normally distributed, with most people scoring in the middle range of these scales, that of psychoticism is highly skewed, with most people positioned at the stable end of the dimension. A high score on the P scale does not mean that the person is psychotic but it means that they are vulnerable to psychosis when under stress. It is also thought that the P scale measures something broader than proneness to psychosis since criminals, alcoholics, drug addicts all have high P scores, something more like social deviance in general. Eysenck's research has not yet found an anatomical location for psychoticism.

There are several criticisms of the Eysenckian approach to personality. First there is too much emphasis upon biological aspects determining personality at the expense of other factors; behaviour is often a result of the social situation. Second, Eysenck's descriptions tend to explain behaviour on the basis of a few dimensions which almost results in stereotyping individuals. To what extent are people consistently introverted or consistently extroverted? Third, Eysenck's questionnaires are devised to allow only yes/no answers; there is no room for the respondent to explain any of his/her decisions and choices which may influence the interpretation of results. Further, people are not necessarily consistent so the administration of a personality questionnaire can only indicate certain things about a person at a particular time and in a given situation. Generalisations and predictions about a person's personality and behaviour are debatable. Fourth, Eysenck suggested that most people fall somewhere in the middle of each dimension, but, if the majority of the population are clustered in the centre, is the theory much use for telling us more about personality when it is essentially concerned with individual differences?

Freud (1856-1939) emphasised that heredity lays a basic maturational pattern, but the personality one develops is determined by the experiences one has in each of these maturational stages. In effect, the physiology of a person sets the limits within which the environment and experience can influence the development of personality.

Freud saw behaviour as being purposeful and goal directed towards satisfying internal drives, needs and desires. These biological drives, mainly sexual in nature, are hereditarily rooted within the body and pass through certain stages of development. Freud also believed that persons had a conscious and unconscious mind and that the unconscious mind in particular was the driving force behind much of behaviour. For Freud, the unconscious mind was structurally organised into three main parts: the id, ego and superego. At birth psychic energy rests with the id. It is the original source of personality and consists of a mass of impulses or instinctual drives lacking in any directing or guiding consciousness. The id is entirely unconscious, amoral and not subject to the external realities. As the instinctual drives and energies increase, the id functions in such a way as to release the pressures and somehow obtain satisfaction. The id, therefore, indulges in immediate and selfish satisfaction corresponding to the pleasure principle, "I want what I want and I want it now." By contrast, the ego is conscious of both internal and external stimuli and so functions in accordance with the reality principle. The ego takes the role of the arbitrator. Its main function is to balance the internal appetites of the id with the external realities of the world in the hope of obtaining some kind of equilibrium. The ego develops the socialised self and the more this ego develops the less energy there is for the id and all its desires. The superego absorbs the social and cultural values presented to it and in this way establishes a code of moral principles and conduct. Interestingly, some claims have been made that an underdeveloped superego leads to criminal and juvenile delinquency.

Freud believed that the all-important years for the formation of personality were during childhood and adolescence, and these early experiences were the key to later development and continually influenced behaviour throughout life. If there are problems for the child/adolescent at any particular stage, then there will be a **fixation** at that stage. For instance, if a child fails to achieve satisfaction at the 'oral stage' then as an adult he/she may smoke.

Freud contrived five stages of development which are based on the three main orifices of the body.

The oral stage is subdivided into the oral-erotic (0–8 months) and the oral-sadistic (6–18 months) substages. The erotic areas here are the mouth, lips, tongue, and later the teeth, jaws, skin and sense organs. The mode of obtaining pleasure initially, is passive incorporation (receiving) and later, active incorporation (seizing). Frustrations are likely to be caused by the lack of mother due to weaning and the birth of new children. If problems have arisen during this period, then adult personality characteristics are likely to include many activities associated with the mouth (e.g. smoking, food faddism, over-eating etc.), demandingness and clingingness; the 'dependent personality'.

The anal stage is subdivided into the anal-sadistic (8 – 24 months) and the anal-erotic (0 – 4 years) substages. The erotic areas are the anus, buttocks and musculature system. The mode of obtaining pleasure, initially, is eliminative and, subsequently, retentive. Frustrations are likely to be toilet training and other demands for self-control. Adult characteristics stemming from this period include bossiness, assertiveness, orderliness, stubbornness and over-punctuality; 'obsessional/compulsive personality'.

The phallic stage (3 – 6 years) views the erotic areas as the genitalia and pleasure is mainly masturbatory. The child becomes very attracted to the opposite-sex parent. Frustrations result in: for the male, the Oedipus complex (and castration complex); for the female, the Electra complex (and penis envy). If this stage is successfully completed then the child will have developed a 'superego' through 'identifying' with the same-sex parent; the child will adopt that parent's moral rule as being the best way to behave in the world. Failure to resolve the complex will lead to poor superego development and possible delinquency.

The latency stage (5 – 12 years) is where the libidinal (sexual) energy becomes desexualised and redirected to outside parental surrogates (especially teachers) and same-sex peers. Frustrations can include inferiority in competitive achievement and social rejection by peers, leading to adult feelings of inferiority, over-competitiveness and over-co-operation.

The genital stage is from the onset of the development of secondary sexual characteristics. The object becomes the opposite sex of the same age and outside the family. If all previous stages have been satisfactorily completed, the individual will now be able to love others and to act unselfishly (but virtually nobody, Freud stresses, reaches this state entirely).

Freudian theory has been the subject of much criticism. For example, his notions of the id, ego and superego are abstract concepts which cannot be located within the body unless, of course, the mind is seen to equate with the brain. The theory does not explain personality differences. For instance, why is it that two people who have gone through the same experiences do not necessarily develop the same adult problems or neuroses. It may well be the case that adult experiences, rather than childhood experiences, influence the individual to be compulsive or independent. Despite these criticisms, Freud's reference to psychological defence mechanisms, like repression and denial, can be exceptionally useful and something of which health professionals should be aware.

The following psychological defence mechanisms are internal adjustments enabling us to cope with unpleasant situations and emotions like anxiety, illness and death. They are often unconscious, psychological processes, automatically enacted to reduce or avoid threat and danger. They are usually adaptive and necessary in a real world but, if they are exaggerated or used persistently, may lead to maladaptive behaviour and experiences in both patients and health professionals.

A mechanism may reduce anxiety by changing an individual's perception of the situation. A common example is **denial** where a person manages to remain unaware of the anxiety provoking situation. Some patients who have suffered heart attacks can, in this way, minimise the anxiety and remain calm. This can be beneficial. There is evidence that patients who deny feeling frightened or apprehensive in the coronary care unit for the first few days have better survival rates than those patients who admit their fear. However, too much denial during recovery may interfere with a patient's willingness or ability to follow treatment procedures. **Denial** may also be used by the health professional, particularly if dealing with very serious conditions. In this case it may manifest itself in an optimistic attitude of the health professional and this may help the patient to cope.

Excessive denial, however, may strain the trust that should develop between the patient and the health professional.

Displacement occurs when thoughts or feelings are directed away from the emotionally significant person and instead are projected on to another person: a health professional who has been criticised by his superior may become angry with his/her patient; or patients may behave abusively towards you because they feel they have been insulted by some other health professional.

Projection occurs when unacceptable feelings and thoughts within oneself are attributed to and perceived as belonging to someone else. A patient may insist that there is nothing wrong and is only seeking help because his/her partner is upset about his/her symptoms. In another case, a patient who has developed erotic feelings toward the health professional may accuse him/her of making sexual advances. A health professional who is uncomfortable about discussing a patient's condition may feel that the patient doesn't really want to know.

Constriction of awareness is a process whereby the person reduces his/her sphere of awareness to exclude unpleasant situations from consciousawareness. This is usually achieved by focusing all attention on some limited aspect of life, e.g. a burns patient may focus exclusively on his pain to avoid becoming aware of the possibility of being seriously disfigured.

At the cognitive level, it is the processing of the incoming information that is being distorted. **Repression** is the mechanism that underlies the forgetting of unpleasant things – it bars unwanted impulses, memories, desires, thoughts and feelings from the consciousness. But these feelings and impulses don't cease to exist and under some circumstances this may be revealed, e.g. during hypnosis or sleep we may think of doing things we wouldn't normally entertain if we were conscious. Under the influence of drugs, severe fatigue or fever, normally unacceptable impulses and behaviour (e.g. obscene language or 'improper suggestions') may be expressed. Other more common behaviours that may also indicate repression include the forgetting of medical appointments, forgetting details about symptoms and then forgetting to take medication.

Rationalisation is the process whereby the person explains away the anxiety-provoking situation, e.g. shortness of breath is explained as an allergy to something (rather than smoking too much).

Intellectualisation is similar to rationalisation in that it uses intellectual processors to cope with anxiety-provoking situations. Some patients may spend much of their time reading about their condition in medical journals and text books. Understanding a condition in some way implies mastery of it. This is probably an effective defence mechanism and should be encouraged by health professionals.

Isolation is the process whereby the patient is able to disassociate himself/herself from the memories/feelings that we think would be painful to recall. Patients may be able to describe in detail painful experiences, accidents, crashes etc., without becoming overly emotional.

Fantasy allows us to achieve some gratification of wishes and desires that are difficult to satisfy in reality. They also serve to distract us from unpleasant situations. For some, physical examination may satisfy unfulfilled sexual needs; for others, being the centre of attention or being cared for may be enough. Some patients may even seek to gratify masochistic urges through repeated requests for painful treatments. It should be understood that many of the wishes are unconscious.

Behaviour itself can be used as a means of psychological defence. **Counterphobic responses** refers to the process by which a person exposes himself/herself to the very situations he/she fears. An example here might be the cancer patient who forms a group to raise money for cancer research, or the alcoholic who chooses to serve drink in a bar.

Withdrawal is a means by which a person avoids the occurrence of painful emotions by declining to engage in old/new interpersonal relationships. Some patients stop interpersonal contact after being informed of a serious condition. They fear immediate or later social rejection and this is their way of dealing with it.

Regression is a defence mechanism which leads to the person returning to a child-like state. It can sometimes be observed in patients suffering from medical and psychopathological conditions. Since the patient is expected to entrust his/her life and welfare to others, he/she must assume a child-like dependent role. This can lead to problems because the patient no longer takes responsibility for his/her own health.

Identification is the taking on of the characteristics of another person. It may act as a defence mechanism in several ways. Separation from a loved one can cause anxiety, but this can be reduced if you become like your loved one, taking on their attitudes, values and manner. A patient may also identify with the person who is looking after them, in this way gaining some of their power and ability. Students in the health professions may identify with their tutor, using them as role models for their own behaviour, not always with desirable consequences.

Personality influences an individual's reactions to illness and injury, and the willingness with which he/she assumes the sick role. Although each person has his/her own unique personality, it is sometimes useful in the context of health care to classify patients according to loosely defined 'personality types'. The value in identifying these Eysenckian-type personalities is that it may help us to understand the meaning of illness or injury for the given patient and, in turn, its influence on sick-role performance. This understanding can then provide the rationale for developing optimal ways of interacting with the patient. Without it, confusion and misunderstanding can develop between a "difficult" patient and the health care personnel. Patients may tentatively be categorised in the following way:

The **dependent, demanding** patients have a need for a great deal of reassurance, and often want special attention from health care personnel. They tend to become dependent on the health professionals and often make frequent, inappropriately urgent calls. When their (excessive) demands are not met, they feel angry and rejected, and are likely to perceive the health care as cold and uncaring. In extreme cases, the patient may regress to an almost infantile state of dependency.

The **orderly, controlling** patients are motivated by a desire to control external and internal states. Behind this desire to control may be the fear of loss of control that may come with illness or injury. Such patients tend not to show feelings and generally experience symptoms without outward signs of emotional reaction. These patients will have difficulty adopting the sick role; they may feel deeply threatened by the control that health professionals must assume over their lives and bodies in order to administer medical care. They may respond by becoming contentious, complaining, and accusatory. They may become incensed and highly critical if appointments or treatments are delayed. They need detail and facts and, therefore, don't respond well to blanket reassurances. To this end, detailed explanations of the diagnosis, the physical and laboratory findings and treatment plans should be given; it may even be useful to ask the patient to keep a record or diary of his symptoms and treatments. What you are doing is giving the patient a degree of control over his/her own care.

The **dramatising, emotional** patients tend to be rather charming and fun to talk with. They have a certain flair and are often quite amusing. They may be overtly seductive, tending to consider their relationship with the health professional as special and with sexual overtones. Split reactions to this type of patient are common, some staff liking them and others becoming rather angry with them. This type of person appears to have a very strong need to be attractive and desirable to others, and a deep fear of rejection, accentuated by their illness. What we are seeing in their behaviour is an exaggerated need to be reassured that they are still attractive and will not be deserted. This type of patient cooperates best if the health professional responds within set boundaries and limits, showing some warmth and personal contact; repeated reassurances are usually all that is required. The personal manner of the health professional is probably more important to this patient than factual information concerning his/her condition and treatment, i.e. it is not what you say but the way that you say it that provides the reassurance in this case.

The **long suffering, self-sacrificing** patients are those who often speak in wailing, complaining voices; their history involves a long list of hard-luck stories and disasters, treatments that didn't work or went wrong, promised cures for symptoms bringing on more symptoms and side effects, protracted pain and suffering; they almost believe they have been born to suffer. It has been suggested that the underlying dynamic in these patients involves strong feelings of guilt that do not allow them to enjoy life or themselves. It is almost as if they have a need to suffer in order to expiate the guilt feelings. Another suggestion is that these patients use pain and suffering as a means of maintaining interpersonal relationships. The attention given to them by relatives and health care personnel is rewarding for them and encourages the sick-role response. This type of patient can often create several problems for the health care team. Typically, they tend to react negatively to reassurances and treatment, totally frustrating the health professional. The patient often believes that the treatment isn't working, or even that it is doing more harm than good. Sometimes they may attribute this to bad luck but at other times they may say they are being mistreated. This frequently results in rejection by the health professional which only adds to the patients feelings of mistreatment. This in turn may lead to feelings of guilt in the health professional. Dealing with this type of patient involves the health professional recognising the necessity of accepting and setting limited goals; giving the patients credit for the way they handle their suffering; expressing appreciation for their courage and perseverance. It would be a mistake to promise these patients complete relief from their pain and suffering; this would only leave them feeling exposed and helpless, without any means of relating to others.

The **guarded, suspicious** patients are always watchful and concerned about the possibility that harm might be done to them, intentionally or unintentionally. They are likely to misinterpret statements and actions, reading something ominous or threatening into them. These patients tend to blame others for their condition or lack of progress in their treatment. They don't enjoy the sick role; they feel fearful and vulnerable and this makes co-operation with health care personnel difficult for them. It is easy for the health professionals themselves to feel threatened by these suspicions and lack of trust; this must be avoided. It is best to assume a neutral attitude concerning these suspicions, criticisms and even outright hostility; avoid being drawn into argument. It can sometimes help to put the blame for the suspicious on to impersonal things like regulations. Above all, of course, you should provide little cause for suspicion; you should be consistent in your statements and behaviour; you should try to keep the patient well informed about his/her condition and treatment by providing as much explanation and information as is feasible.

Patients thinking of themselves as **superior** or **special** have a tendency to appear snobbish, self-confident and arrogant. These patients often have idealised body images and their illness or condition represents a threat to that body image. They do not find the sick role agreeable; it contradicts the notions of perfection that they feel about themselves. They don't like the idea that they are not competent to help themselves and they are likely to show open resentment towards those members of the health care team that they feel are inferior. It is hardly surprising that this type of patient is not very popular! The first step in dealing with this type of person is in acknowledging this aspect of the patient's personality; allowing the patient his/her feelings of superiority, his/her boasts, while maintaining an attitude of security about one's own professional competence will help to reduce potential conflict.

The **seclusive, aloof** patients seem to be remote, detached and not in need of any interpersonal contact. They often prefer to be by themselves and seldom speak to other patients or staff members. They prefer solitary activities like reading or listening to music. The patient probably lives like this normally and the relatively public sick role that he/she is required to adopt in hospital may be quite uncomfortable or threatening. It is important to recognise and respect this need for privacy when interacting with this type of person; attempts to increase their social responsiveness will probably not be welcomed (Barry, 1989).

The implications for the health professional are that understanding the patient's personality can help to formulate an optimal approach to the patient. The health professional should also be aware of their own personality and how this may produce a conflict in a health care setting. For example, if you feel that you are an orderly controlling type of person, you may find yourself challenged and your ability questioned by a patient who has a similar personality. Keeping at a distance from the situation emotionally when such conflicts arise and understanding the personality needs of the patient can help the health professional avoid becoming entangled in unnecessary personality conflicts.

Environmental approaches to personality relate to the nurture side of the nature/nurture debate. Unlike Sheldon and Eysenck who place great emphasis upon biological and inherited characteristics, these theories view personality as more changeable, more fluid and less static. Personality is held to be learnt as a result of our experiences.' Social learning theory' and 'self and role theories' are two approaches to personality that fall under the banner of environmental approaches.

Social learning theory is based on the principles of behaviourism; that is, an individual learns when he/she is rewarded for doing something and when pleasurable consequences follow a response to a specific stimulus. With this theory, personality is assumed to begin with reflexes and innate drives, such as hunger and thirst, to which the individual learns to respond. Beyond these initial reflexes, personality and behaviour is seen to be a result of the learning processes that each of us experience. These learning processes occur through imitation, having behaviour rewarded, reinforced and sometimes punished.

Social learning theory can be criticised on the grounds that little attention is paid to the biological and genetic determinants of personality and behaviour. Personality is generally thought to be more stable than this theory advocates. The question must be asked, "Why do individuals learn some things but not others?" For example, "Why do some children continue to smoke although aversive consequences follow?" The theory only explains some aspects of behaviour and, when it does, these fragmented aspects are fairly simple.

Broadly speaking, **self and role theories** suggest that personality develops as a result of reacting and thinking as we believe other people want and expect us to react and think.

Role theory, as proposed by Goffman (1959) implies that personality is no more than the sum total of all the roles that an individual has played or is playing. An individual plays various roles as he/she goes through life, each with their own set of expectations.
Interestingly, studies have shown that when people are asked, "Who am I?", fifty percent of the answers tend to be in role terms. However, role theory has its criticisms. The theory does not adequately deal with the notion of role conflict, for instance, in the role of a nurse an individual may be expected to participate in either electroconvulsive therapy for a mentally ill person or in abortion procedures. These occupational expectations may conflict with personal values and attitudes in a non-occupational or non-nurse capacity. Is it the case that some roles are more dominant than others? Are occupational roles chosen to suit personality or does personality determine choice of occupational role?

Self theories of personality hold the self-concept as being central to what is meant by personality. Laing distinguished between a **true** self which is akin to a private self and a **false** self which is the self presented for social purposes and the one that attempts to match the expectations placed upon us. Rogers differentiated between the **ideal** self, that is what one would like to be, and the **actual** self which is what one is really like.

Cooley's (1902) 'looking glass theory' states, "the self that is most important is a reflection, largely from the minds of others". In other words, our self-concept is derived from what we think other people think about us. The self-concept is an important personhood feature and will be discussed in more detail in the next chapter. Nevertheless, there is an important question raised by the self theory of personality: is personality no more than the internalisation of the expectations of others?

Discussion Points

1. Can changes in personality be brought about through illness, injury, treatment or hospitalisation?

2. Are certain personalities better able to cope with illness?

3. Can you see how any of the above theories are useful in understanding the personalities of the patients with whom you come into contact?

4. Are some personalities more suitable for nurse education?

5. Does nursing education change personality in any way?

6. What is the role of the health professional?

7. What expectations are placed upon the health professional?

8. What is the sick role?

9. What are the rights, duties and expectations of the sick role?

10. Why do some individuals accept the sick role more readily than others?

Useful Reading

Barry, P.D., (1989). *Psychosocial Nursing*, Lippincott
Coleman, J.C., (1977). *Introductory Psychology*, Routledge & Kegan Paul
Dobson C.B. & Hardy, M. *et al.* (1988). *Understanding Psychology*, Weidenfeld & Nicholson
Gross, R., (1989). *Psychology: The Science of Mind and Behaviour*, Hodder & Stoughton
Medcof, J. & Roth, J., (1978). *Approaches to Psychology*, The Open University Press

Chapter 7
The perception of illness and its influence upon our self-concept

Perception is not the same as sensation which implies the simple registration of stimuli on our sense organs. Perception is a higher-level cognitive function which enables us to select, process and interpret information about our environment. It enables us to make sense of and attach meaning to whatever we experience. Perception is a selective process because we can only attend to so many pieces of information at any one time in a particular context. Not only is perception influenced by what we choose to focus our attention on, but it is also affected by past experience and our memory of those previous experiences, by our personalities, our needs, our expectations, values, the ways in which we think and communicate.

The question arises, "What stimuli do we select to focus attention on in relation to illness and health?" What factors are we taking into account when we say that we are ill or healthy; what signs, symptoms and feelings are we attending to and which ones are we ignoring? A research study revealed that one in five elderly people who deemed themselves to be in poor health had general practitioners who perceived them to be in good health. Conversely, two out of three elderly people who were rated as being in poor health by their doctors thought of themselves as being in good health. So what differentiated the perceptions and who was more right in their interpretation? This is not a simple issue, essentially because perception is a subjective and individualised way of viewing the world and experience within the world, and because the concepts of illness and health themselves are complex.

On one level, a concept of health appears to be universal but, on another level, it needs to be acknowledged that not every person, society or culture pursues the same means to achieve health. For instance, one person may equate health with fitness, another may view health as being free from disease or pain whilst someone else will claim that health entails the prevention of disease. Clear definitions of health are extremely difficult to pin down. The concept of health is best thought of in relative terms; that is, its meaning is dependent upon how the individual perceives it. We cannot measure how healthy one is feeling because health involves taking into account biological, psychological and social influences upon the person.

Similarly, the concept of illness is complex and difficult to define. On one level, a concept of illness equates with ideas of disease and pain but, on another level, it also implies a discontinuity in health. Given that feeling healthy is an individual decision it follows that feeling ill is also an individual decision dependent upon biological, psychological and social influences. These three types of influences need to be seen as interactive in the sense that what may appear to be biological or physiological in origin may well be the result of psychological or social pressures, and vice versa. For example, psychological stress can exacerbate angina or lead to cardiac palpitations; conversely, the diagnosis of cancer may lead to the person relinquishing his/her occupational role which might, in turn, diminish self-respect and result in feelings of worthlessness.

The interrelationships between the biological, psychological and social influences upon the perception of illness is further evidenced in that a person's own theory of illness is likely to be characterised by these same three dimensions. For example, a person may experience bodily sensations or changes and/or possess information based upon previous experience of illness and/or receive information from the social world; these internal and external sources can all aid interpretation of illness. The interactive nature of the biological, psychological and social influences upon illness, is also reflected in how the health care team manage illness: for instance, the biological management of illness rests upon operations, the administration of drugs, physiotherapy etc; the psychological management of illness may require effective communication and counselling; and the social management of illness is likely to involve social support, home visits, help from family and friends, etc.

All of these factors, coupled with the expectations that people have about illness contribute to the creation of the sick role. The sick role is embedded in social rights and duties. The patient is usually excused from duties, such as work, and is expected to feel uncomfortable or to be in pain and to co-operate with the health care professionals. The patient is generally perceived to have less responsibility, others reduce their expectations of the patient and he/she receives attention. At the same time, however, the patient is seen to be responsible for getting better as quickly as possible and, in the first instance, for seeking and following medical advice. Nevertheless, the problems of illness and the subsequent sick role are not always as clear cut. For example, it is not easy for a person who is extremely depressed to 'pull him/herself together' and want to get better. Further, not everyone will recognise or acknowledge that they are ill; therefore, expecting that person to fulfil the sick role readily is probably a somewhat naive expectation.

The sick role and perception of illness are influenced by several idiosyncratic factors; the background of the individual, social class, age, sex and ethnicity will confound the issue. A person's tolerance or threshold for pain will vary and, therefore, determine the amount of time taken before seeking medical advice. A person may be anxious about certain signs and symptoms because they fear time off work and loss of earnings. The social desirability of the illness is also a factor to consider. For example, the occurrence of syphilis may lead a person to deny the signs and symptoms and, in turn, refuse to seek treatment. According to Kent and Dalgleish (1983), social factors do, indeed, influence whether a person disregards or attends to the signs and symptoms of illness. Whatever the signs and symptoms, they require internal analysis by the person. An important consideration lies with the information that persons select, process and interpret. Kent and Dalgleish remark that persons need to reduce their uncertainty and anxiety about signs and symptoms and often hypothesise about the possible explanations. They also suggest that the difficulty involved in attempting to interpret signs and symptoms is a significant factor with regard to why people delay seeking help or medical advice. Imboden (1972) supports this in the sense of claiming that people tend to deny the onset of more insidious illness. Similarly, Lipowski (1975) points out that a gradual onset of illness is inadequately attended to.

Psychological factors play a significant role in the way persons experience and perceive illness and the symptoms. Not only can psychological factors induce illness symptoms but they can also mask them. The classic example is when an individual feels ill, decides to consult the doctor and as soon as he/she enters the surgery the illness symptoms disappear. Lynch *et al.* (1974) refer to the person who had an intermittent atrial/ventricular (AV) block. Whenever a nurse took the woman's pulse the missing of a particular heart beat did not occur, but as soon as the nurse left the coronary unit the heart started to miss a beat once again. Pennebaker (1984) reaffirms that perception is dependent upon external and internal information that requires attending to and suggests that when the external environment is lacking in information or failing to provide any clues as to why we feel as we do, then we are more likely to place emphasis upon internal information. Similarly, if we are particularly concerned with and engrossed in events taking place in the external environment, then we are inclined to disregard internal factors. For instance, it is usually easier to forget or be unaware of headache, toothache and some degree of pain if we are otherwise preoccupied.

The perception of illness and its influence upon our self-concept

Awareness of ourselves in biological, psychological and social terms is important for the development of the self-concept. More specifically, our own body image, how we think of ourselves and how we think other people perceive us influences the concept that we have of the self. Much of the meaning that we attach to the self derives essentially from private experiences. Each one of us believes that we are distinct and separate from other people, essentially because we all live inside our own heads and recognise the privacy of our own consciousness. For example, it is through internal communication, that is, communicating with ourselves our own thoughts and feelings, that we learn to communicate with others, perhaps in the sense of externalising or expressing those thoughts and feelings. Sometimes it is easier to communicate with the self than it is with others. Further, internal thoughts and feelings can remain secret and safeguarded. The notion of experience enhances the idea of a self-concept because it is seen to relate to ourselves: our personal world of experience which to some degree has boundaries since we make decisions as to what concerns us and what doesn't. The self-concept implies an element of continuity: we have a history and a biography which enables us to view our past, present and future. The self-concept involves thinking of ourselves as 'causes' of events, situations and circumstances; we maintain that we behave intentionally and purposefully and accept, in part, responsibility for our choices, actions and consequences. However, we also assume that we are very much like other people in that we all share similar subjective experiences; we also reflect upon, comment on, analyse and summarise the experiences of the self. In this sense then we also define the self by comparing it to others.

The self-concept is actually quite difficult to define, primarily because of the extensive range of adjectives that have been attached to the term self. For instance, self-esteem, self-awareness, self-image, self-conscious, self-acceptance and self-actualisation. There are numerous definitions and interpretations of the self-concept; hence it is only possible to refer to a selection.

Murphy (1947) suggested that "the self is the individual as known to the individual." Allport (1955) claimed "The first aspect we encounter is the bodily me." Feeling and being affected by our own body leads us to separate the self from the external world. This seems to be supported by Piaget's view that during the sensorimotor stage the child gradually distinguishes him/herself from the outside world. Body image is often an important factor for the social self-concept, for example great height for a young adolescent may lead to a negative self-concept and embarrassment because all his/her peers are so much smaller.

Kuhn (1960) has shown that as we grow older the self-concept becomes less concerned with the body image and increasingly dependent upon positive feedback and validation from others in relation to being socially acceptable. Goffman (1959) considers that the self-concept is bound up with the notion of roles. He suggests that in order to effectively perform a new role a person puts on a mask to give the impression of possessing the qualities required. If the role is played for long enough it will become an integral part of the self-concept. Mead (1956) believed the self-concept to arise only through social experience because the self is a product of those social experiences. He argued that an individual is concerned about how other people perceive him/her, and, to enable the individual to anticipate the responses of other people, he/she learns to perceive and interpret the social world in the same way as they do. Secord and Backman (1974) propose that the self-concept comprises three aspects. First, a **cognitive** component representing descriptive judgements about the self, for example, I am tall, slim and have blue eyes. Second, an **affective** component representing one's feelings about the self which might include a general self evaluation as well as specific judgements, for example, "I am basically honest but tend to be a hypochondriac." Third, a **behavioural** component which is indicative of the way an individual might act towards the self, for example, I am self-indulgent.

The perception of illness and its influence upon our self-concept

According to Burns (1981), the self-concept consists of two essential parts: self-image and self-esteem. **Self-image** is constructed from beliefs about oneself, from life experience and feedback from others. Negative feedback from others can result in a negative self-image, just as positive feedback can encourage a positive self-image. However, the question arises, "If the self-image is dependent upon, in part, feedback from others, then do we always select, process and interpret information correctly?" Do we at times misconstrue what other people are saying and meaning? For instance, feed-back can easily be perceived to be negative when it was meant to be positive, and vice versa.

Self-esteem, according to Burns, is based upon how we evaluate each aspect of our self-image, how we judge our beliefs about ourselves. For example, incorporated into an individual's self-image may be the belief that he/she has a high pain threshold and tolerance of pain. The individual's evaluation of this belief might entail thinking that this is positive since he/she does not complain and is not seen to be attention-seeking. On the other hand, it can be negative because important signs and symptoms underpinning the pain may be masked, ignored or unattended to.

Burns concludes that it is the combination of these beliefs and evaluations about the self, that is, the interrelationship between the self-image and self-esteem, which constitutes the self-concept and, in turn, links it to attitudes. Attitudes can be defined as evaluated beliefs that influence the person to behave and perceive in particular ways. In effect, the self-concept could be interpreted as a plurality of attitudes towards oneself in a range of social contexts.

Discussion Points

1. What sorts of illness symptoms do you attend to or ignore?

2. How might a health professional's perception of a hospital or clinic differ from that of a patient's?

3. Do you ever perceive just what you want to perceive?

4. How might a person's bodily injuries influence his/her perception of him/herself and how might other people perceive those same injuries and the injured person?

5. What is your own self-concept?

6. Do we have one self-concept or several?

Useful Reading

Baum, A. & Taylor S.E., (1984). *Handbook of Psychology and Health*, Earlbaum

Burns, R.B., (1981). *Essential Psychology*, MTP Press

Kent & Dalgleish, (1986). *Psychology and Medical Care*, Balliere Tindall

Lloyd, A. & Mayes, P., (1984). *Introduction to Psychology*, Fontana

Secord, P.F. & Backman, C.N., (1974). *Social Psychology*, McGraw Hill

Skevington, S., (eds.) (1984). *Understanding Nurses: The Social Psychology of Nurses*, Wiley & Son

Chapter 8
Intelligence: Does it decline with age?

The term 'intelligence' is another key psychological concept that defies a universally acceptable definition because its understanding and interpretation is dependent upon individual, social and cultural factors as well as the idiosyncratic preferences and beliefs of those theorists who attempt to explain the term. Intelligence relates to the nature/nurture debate, that is, intelligence can be seen as innate potential, as determined by the opportunities for learning or as influenced by the interaction of potential and learning.

There are numerous definitions of intelligence. The following few provide an overview of how the term has been referred to:

- Cyril Burt claimed intelligence to be "innate general cognitive thinking." Burt even went so far as to attribute 80% of intelligence to heredity/nature and 20% to the environment/nurture. How he actually arrived at these figures is somewhat questionable, particularly since quantifying and measuring an abstract complex term like intelligence is difficult and perhaps impossible.

- Heim held that intelligence is "the ability to grasp at essentials and respond appropriately to them."

- For Ryle, intelligence is being able to apply what has been learned to new situations.

- Whitbourne and Weinstock define adult intelligence as the "overall integration of the basic cognitive processes of perception, psychomotor reactions and learning with the higher order cognitive processes of conceptualisation, reasoning and abstract symbolisation."

If these definitions lead to dissatisfaction then it is likely that Boring's definition will be seen to be equally inadequate. Boring claimed that "intelligence is what intelligence tests measure." This kind of claim is fallacious because no two tests measure exactly the same thing, so that one is left with as many definitions of intelligence as there are tests.

Can intelligence be measured? The psychometric approach in psychology would attempt such a task. This quantitative approach views intelligence as a combination of various abilities and that each of these abilities can be measured separately, for example, verbal skills, comprehension, mathematical and perceptual skills. One of the central questions in mind is, "What aspects of mental functioning distinguish more intelligent people from the less intelligent?" The basic idea, in order to measure these individual differences, is to have people perform a number of tasks that seem to identify intelligent functioning or predict future intelligent performance. A classic example of this is the 11+ examination, whereby the test scores were used to determine whether an individual would do well at grammar school or would be better suited to a place in a secondary modern school.

Intelligence: Does it decline with age?

The first intelligence test was developed by Binet (1905), who wanted to find a measure of the kind of abilities which so obviously differentiated people in daily life and which differentiated people of different ages. It is claimed that as children get older they can solve problems of increasing difficulty. By looking at the age at which a child first solves a problem we gain some understanding of the difficulty level of that problem. Children, as a result of intelligence testing, are given a mental age, for example, an eight-year-old may be able to solve problems typically solved by twelve-year-olds; hence his/her mental age would be twelve. The ratio between mental age and chronological age, expressed as a percentage, gives us the term intelligent quotient (IQ).

$$\text{So} \quad IQ \quad \frac{\textit{Mental age:}}{\textit{Chronological Age:}} \times 100 = \frac{12 \times 100}{8} = 150$$

A 'normal' or average IQ is approximately 100. It is generally held that mildly mentally handicapped persons have an IQ of about 50–70; scores below 50 are considered to be subnormal. Shanley (1986) remarked that the policy of segregation in the 18th and 19th centuries, that is, accommodating 'sick' people in the workhouses, fuelled the idea that, as less-intelligent people tended to marry less-intelligent people and, therefore, produce less-intelligent children, then eventually there would be a decline in the intelligence of the population generally because these people procreate at a much faster rate. These misguided beliefs influenced the government of the 1930s who went so far as to consider compulsory sterilisation for the mentally handicapped. Nazi Germany far exceeded these considerations and actually exterminated those people perceived to have unacceptable and undesirable characteristics. In 1951 a report found that twenty-one states in the USA practised sterilisation on the mentally handicapped on the basis of their IQ scores.

Where there is evidence of cognitive deficit due to brain damage or dysfunction, or some kind of genetic disorder, mentally handicapped persons usually score lower on IQ tests than those with other forms of mental handicap, and no amount of experience can change this. However, with less severe forms of mental handicap, intellectual competence, though still limited, can be improved. Mental handicap may have restricted the individual's opportunity for learning through little schooling, limited social contact with a variety of people and less experience of different social environments. This point brings us back to the nature/nurture debate. Although the evidence is not conclusive, some studies have given strong support to the idea that genetics or heredity influences intelligence. Research on intelligence and monozygotic twins suggests that any similarities in intelligence between the twins, when separated and brought up in 'truly' different environments, is due to nature, that is, they are genetically identical. The problem here lies with the notion of what constitutes a truly different environment and how these differences and their effects on intelligence are measured. Other research supports the idea that nurture or environmental factors influence the development of intelligence. Clarke and Clarke (1958) noted large increases in intelligence in supposedly mentally subnormal young adults who had been institutionalised for a few months. They concluded that the increase in intelligence (increased IQ score) represented recovery from early adversity. The individuals who made the largest gains in intelligence were those from the worst backgrounds who had frequently experienced cruelty and gross neglect. This study was important for two main reasons. First, it showed that the quality of experience is very for important for intellectual growth. Mental subnormality has many reasons and 'causes', including a poor environment. The prognosis is much better for those individuals whose subnormality is related to adverse early experience as opposed to brain dysfunction. Second, it indicated that intellectual growth does not stop at a particular age, that nature does not set rigid time limits and boundaries on the effects of experience.

The link between intelligence and **social class** is an area on which several researchers have focused their attention. One study claimed an IQ of twenty points difference between children from professional parents and children from unskilled manual parents. White and Watt (1973) found that middle class mothers spend more time interacting with their children, particularly in terms of naming and explaining things. They also found that these mothers encouraged up to three times more activity than they discouraged, unlike working class mothers whom they described as more discouraging of activity than encouraging, and much more controlling.

Intelligence and **race** has been researched by Jensen who claimed a difference of fifteen IQ points between samples of American black and American white individuals. He concluded that inherited characteristics accounted for the difference and that black people were inferior to white people because of their inability to reason abstractly. Similarly, Tyler (1965) studied black people in North and South America and made the claim that southern black people were less intelligent. The criticism that can be levelled at research of this nature is that it ignores any environmental influences, for instance, social inequalities and lack of opportunity in education, employment and housing.

The relationship between intelligence and **age** concentrates on the question of what happens to intelligence as we grow older? Until recent years, psychologists believed that intelligence declined steadily after peak performance in the early 20s. This kind of claim was based on cross-sectional studies where people of different ages were tested on a single occasion and the age differences and age changes commented upon, the general conclusion being that poorer performance occurs in older subjects. Such inferences have subsequently been shown to be unjustified. The use of longitudinal studies, whereby people are tested several times at different ages, have consistently found little or no decrease in intelligence with age.

It seems essential to discuss the concept of ageing prior to any further consideration of the links between ageing and intelligence. In studying human development throughout the lifespan, it is almost impossible to escape the fact that some of the deteriorating consequences of ageing result from an accumulation of defects and failures in the biology of the human body. For example, it is believed there is a reduction in brain weight, that the number of nerve cells decreases and that there may be deposits of plaque in certain areas of the brain which correlate with reduced mental efficiency. There is shrinkage of the skeleton, reduced elasticity of muscles, reduced strength and agility, increased susceptibility to diseases such as rheumatism, cardiovascular disease and respiratory problems. Psychomotor performance may be affected in the sense that fine dexterity, co-ordination, stamina and speed of reaction decline. Mobility may be greatly reduced, coupled with an increased likelihood of falls and accidents. Elderly people may become preoccupied with bodily changes; changes which may affect the self-image and self-esteem and have social consequences like isolation. It would appear to be the case that the physical factors involved in ageing may have psychological and social consequences. It is important to re-emphasise the interactive relationship between physical, psychological and social influences upon the person. Social attitudes and social policies directed towards the elderly can influence how well they adjust to the ageing process, for example, the reduced status of the elderly, diminished finances, insecurity in the face of technology, death of spouse and friends, retirement and an increased difficulty in meeting social needs. Psychological characteristics of the elderly person, such as personality, adaptability, self-concept and motivation, to name but a few, will all influence how ageing is perceived and coped with by the elderly person.

Adapting socially and emotionally to ageing can be considered in the light of two theories: the Theory of Disengagement and the Activity Theory of Ageing.

Disengagement theory (Cummings and Henry, 1961) describes the mutual withdrawal of the elderly and society. As people grow older their social interaction decreases; the decrease is a process characterised by a reciprocal withdrawal between society and the ageing person. This withdrawal has intrinsic developmental qualities as well as responsive ones and is associated with decreased emotional involvement in the activities and social relationships that were important in middle age. The theory states also that, in old age, the individual who has disengaged and who has accordingly reached a new equilibrium characterised by greater psychological distance, altered types of social relationship and decreased social interaction, is the person who has a sense of psychological well-being and is highly satisfied.

Activity Theory (Havinghurst, 1964) suggests that, with the exception of inevitable physical changes, the elderly have the same social and psychological needs as middle-aged people. Any reduced social interaction is seen to be against the will of the individual elderly person. For optimum ageing conditions, elderly people need to stay active and resist the shrinkage of their social world. This theory is really a commonsense view and equates with the view that keeping happy in old age means keeping active. The older person who ages most successfully is the person who stays as active as possible; he/she finds substitutes for activities which have had to be relinquished and substitutes for family and friends lost through death.

It is important to point out, however, that neither theory is true or applicable for all people. These two theories are generalising about the ageing process when it is more important to consider how the individual elderly person perceives his/her own biological, psychological and social state in relation to age.

Old age officially starts around the age of 60–65 years, conveniently linked to retirement which, for most people, excludes them from a part of our cultural heritage and ethos for work. However, applying chronological age to the notion of ageing and the elderly is fallacious and does not necessarily explain individual differences in patterns of cognitive functioning and intellectual competence. One has only to consider practising doctors, judges and politicians over the age of 65 to see that cognitive competence has not declined; we do not have to agree with their decisions and policies, but neither would we claim mental incompetence or suggest that they were unintelligent.

Returning to the use of intelligence testing, ageing older adults do tend to perform less well but this does not mean intelligence declines with age. Intelligence has to be seen to involve personality, memory, learning, education, opportunity, encouragement, challenging job, communication, motivation etc. One of the main issues towards which research has been directed is whether older people have equal difficulty with the acquisition, retention and retrieval of information from memory, or whether some aspects of remembering are easier than others. Wimer and Wigdor (1958) found that the older person who complains of a bad memory may not have forgotten the information in question but failed to learn it properly in the first place. The idea that older people are less efficient learners may well be due to differences in education and other learning experiences rather than age-related decline.

In a series of experiments on memory for spoken texts, Cohen and Faulkner (1981) found that old and young subjects lost non-crucial information at the same rate, but that young subjects were very much better at retaining the core or 'gist' of the story. The old made errors of commission as well as errors of omission, particularly mistakes about who did what. These age differences became apparent when a time delay of forty seconds was used, but were not present when the delay was only ten seconds. Rabbitt and Wright (1980) compared the ability of old and young subjects to monitor and recall sentences spoken either by a single speaker or by more than one speaker. Young subjects could accurately recall a series of four sentences in either condition. Old subjects were able to recall sentence content when this was all that was required. Faced with the additional demand of recalling "who said what", their recall of sentence content, and of speaker, became very poor. Rabbitt also discovered that the old person's own statements may act as a distractor – he/she is less likely to remember the statements of other people when they occur close to his/her own. This task was probably considerably more demanding than ordinary conversations, in which there is often much redundancy of information or surplus cues to meaning, and in which the pace may be adjusted to suit the old person. However, the research does have implications for situations in which older people are being given information which is completely new to them, such as medical information. Cohen (1981) asked older people to make inferences from written statements which were available for review and for which self-pacing was allowed. Errors, relative to the younger group, were reduced under these more favourable conditions, but a residual deficit indicated that inferential reasoning is affected by ageing. A further study looked at comprehension and memory of texts containing explicit or implicit information; the old did almost as well as the young in answering questions about the explicit texts, but were quite poor on texts which required inferences (41% errors compared with 12.5% in the young group).

Perlmutter (1980) suggested that in real-life situations older people often do better at making inferences because they possess more of the general knowledge upon which such inferences must be based. Thus, to the degree that a task depends upon acquired knowledge, older adults will be favoured over younger adults, but, to the degree that it depends on sheer processing capacity, the younger will be favoured.

The idea of acquired knowledge links to Cattell's (1963) distinction between fluid and crystallised intelligence.

Fluid intelligence represents the influence of innate factors rather than being influenced by education and experience. It is the ability to adapt to new situations and is thought to diminish with advancing age. It is similar to Hebb's (1949) notion of Intelligence A: the capacity or potential for development which is carried by the genes.

Crystallised intelligence is something that is built up through experience and is characterised by accumulated and retained knowledge. This type of intelligence has been found to increase over many years and is maintained well into old age. Indeed, it could be argued that the increased wisdom of age and experience compensates for the energy and acquisition of new knowledge in youth, and that wisdom should be included within a definition of intelligence. Crystallised intelligence is similar to Hebb's notion of Intelligence B: the level of intelligence a person currently has as a result of the interaction between a person's innate potential and his/her experience. So Intelligence A plus experience equals Intelligence B, which is similar to what is meant by crystallised intelligence.

In conclusion, intelligence is a rather nebulous concept and one which cannot be defined without reference to a range of cognitive functions like thought, language, problem-solving, learning, memory and perception. These cognitive processes are further confounded by the necessity to take into account the influences of personality, the self-concept, social attitudes and policies, class, sex, race and age.

In this sense, intelligence has to be seen as not static and as something that cannot be measured; it is continually evolving with experience and, at best, can only be assessed and inferred.

So what does all of this information tell the health professional about intelligence and ageing? Bromley (1966, 1974) makes some pertinent statements:

> *"Intelligence is only one factor among many that may influence a person's adjustment to his (her) environment."*

> *".....in old age being well adjusted means being emotionally stable and resourceful in adapting to changed circumstances like bereavement, retirement, ill health ..."*

> *".....a serious disadvantage with psychometric tests is that they may not be applicable, or equally applicable throughout the whole period of adult life and old age...."*

Indeed, the intelligence test does appear to favour the younger person by seeming more relevant. It may be argued that the elderly do less well in tests as they are less motivated in comparison with the young. Young people are more inclined to be competitive and this can carry on into the completion of a test. The young are also accustomed to the continual acquisition of new knowledge. In contrast, the elderly are not necessarily motivated in this way: life consists, to a large extent, in well-maintained routines and repeated skills. However, the occurrence of illness, injury or disability may result in an elderly person having to learn new skills or remember old skills, or cope with complex treatment procedures or be motivated during the rehabilitation stage. In this sense then, the results of intelligence tests may have identified some key areas of functioning which the health professional ought to be aware of when formulating individualised care aimed at matching the intellectual level and needs of the person.

IMPLICATIONS FOR THE HEALTH PROFESSIONAL

1. The older person's activities/learning should be 'self-paced' where possible. Information should be given slowly to allow adequate processing time (i.e. with reasonable gaps between each 'chunk' – a slower **rate** of speaking isn't helpful because it allows more opportunity for distraction **during** reception).

2. Learning by doing or by being shown, rather than having to cope with a mass of verbal instructions, is relatively more helpful to older people than younger ones. This may be partly a generational difference related to educational experiences (and may not apply to subsequent generations of old people) but it is probably also related to reducing the load on short-term memory.

3. Information should be explicit to avoid the need for inferences.

4. One person should give important information, rather than have several 'chipping in', because of the difficulty in processing multi-person conversations.

5. Redundant information should be provided whenever possible, i.e. **several** cues to help the person understand and remember (such as being told to do something at a certain time of day, as part of a regular routine).

6. It is important to make sure that the **wrong** information is not learned – as well as being slower to learn, old people are often also slower to 'unlearn' errors.

7. Messages should be very clear to compensate for the higher sensory thresholds of older people. Distracting stimuli should be minimised.

8. The great variability between older individuals should always be kept in mind. Many people maintain high levels of intellectual functioning, sometimes in spite of ill-health. Even among those showing impairment of function there will be some who simply have inefficient strategies (through disuse of the function in question) and who can benefit from practice, instruction, etc; others may be structurally impaired (cell loss and CNS dysfunction) and less able to benefit from such interventions.

Discussion Points

1. What is your idea of an intelligent person?

2. Have you seen more than one type of intelligence in your dealings with other health professionals?

3. Would it help in your professional role if, at some appropriate time, each of your patients were given an intelligence test?

4. What differences in approach would you use with someone whom you perceived to be highly intelligent compared with a person whom you thought was of limited intelligence?

5. How would you distinguish between intelligence and commonsense – which of these is more important in the field of health care?

Useful Reading

Anastasi, A., (1982). *Psychological Testing*, Macmillan
Bromley, D.B., (1974). *The Psychology of Human Ageing*, Penguin
Fries, J.F. & Crapo, L.M., (1981). *Vitality and Ageing*, Freeman
Hall, J. (ed.), (1982). *Psychology for Nurses and Health Visitors*, Macmillan
Hilgard, E.R. & Atkinson, R.C., (1983). *Introduction to Psychology*, Harcourt, Brace Jovanovich
Kimmel, D.C., (1974). *Adulthood and Ageing: An Interdisciplinary Developmental View*, Wiley
McGhie, A., (1979). *Psychology as Applied to Nursing*, Livingstone
Shanley, E., (1986). *Mental Handicap*, Churchill Livingstone
Sternberg, R.J., & Detterman, D.K. (eds.), (1986). *What is Intelligence? Contemporary Viewpoints on its Nature and Definition*, Norwood

Index